India as a New Global Power

AN ACTION AGENDA FOR THE UNITED STATES

Ashley J. Tellis

India Research Press

India Research Press
B-4/22, Safdarjung Enclave, New Delhi – 110 029.
Ph.: 24694610; Fax : 24618637
www.indiaresearchpress.com
contact@indiaresearchpress.com ; bahrisons@vsnl.com

2005

INDIA AS A NEW GLOBAL POWER
An action agenda for the united states
Ashley J. Tellis

ISBN : 81-8386-000-1

Licensed by , Carnegie Endowment for International Peace
Washington, D.C., USA

Printed in India at Focus Impressions, New Delhi – 110 003.

ACKNOWLEDGMENTS

The author would like to thank Jawed Ashraf, John H. Gill, Neil Joeck, Daniel S. Markey, S. Enders Wimbush, and especially George Perkovich for their thoughtful comments on this report.

CONTENTS

The numerous controversies that swirled around the administration's handling of Iraq during George W. Bush's first term obscured a strategic success with major implications for the future balance of power in Asia: the transformation of relations between the United States and India. Tired of decades of estrangement, President Bush resolved—prior to assuming of.ce in January 2001—that his administration would alter the character of this important bilateral relationship in order to permanently entrench the large, vibrant, and successful democracy that is India in the ranks of U.S. friends and allies.

In Atal Bihari Vajpayee, India's prime minister at the time, Bush found a perfect partner—a statesman who, equally weary of a history of U.S.-Indian antagonism and strongly inclined to regard the United States and India as "natural allies,"1 desired to change New Delhi's strategic direction toward a stronger partnership with Washington.

From 2001 to 2003, the courtship between the United States and India grew in ardor and expectations: Thanks to a series of breakthroughs in bilateral diplomatic collaboration, military-to-military relations, counterterrorism cooperation, and public diplomacy, the way was paved for one of the Bush administration's major .rst-term diplomatic achievements, Next Steps in Strategic Partnership (NSSP). This agreement, which was announced in January 2004 after months of negotiation, drew its inspiration from the Bush-Vajpayee Joint Statement of November 2001.2 It was heralded as a breakthrough in U.S.-Indian strategic collaboration because, despite continuing disagreements on other issues such as trade, Iraq, and the United Nations, it committed both countries to working together in four dif.cult arenas—civilian nuclear energy, civilian space programs, high-technology trade, and missile defense—where India's possession of nuclear weaponry had previously made meaningful cooperation all but impossible.

NSSP AS A HESITANT REVOLUTION

The success of the discussions leading up to NSSP produced connecting claims of paternity in the United States. On the one hand, the Bush administration, and some of its outside partisans, quickly portrayed the new agreement as evidence of how the president had single-handedly transformed the bilateral relationship since taking office in 2001. Several prominent Democrats, on the other hand, ridiculed NSSP in private conversations with their Indian interlocutors, even as they rushed to publicly claim credit for the breakthrough, asserting that it represented little more than an evolutionary outcome of the progressive improvement in U.S.- Indian ties since the last two years of the Clinton administration.

The truth, as usual, lay somewhere between. U.S.-Indian relations certainly experienced an exciting improvement in the final years of the Clinton presidency, beginning with the unequivocal American condemnation of Pakistan's aggression at Kargil and culminating in President Clinton's wildly successful March 2000 visit to India. But these changes primarily represented alterations in atmospherics rather than structural transformations occurring as a result of changes in policy on both sides. In reality, right up to the end of the Clinton administration, U.S.-Indian dealings remained stuck in the same nonproliferation straitjacket that had doomed all efforts at bilateral rapprochement since the initial Indian nuclear test in 1974, with successive administrations in Washington taking the view that India was an inextricable part of the *problem* of proliferation because its nuclear capability and the existence of that capability outside various global regimes made it an obstacle to U.S. nonproliferation efforts internationally. New Delhi's close relationship with the Soviet Union, its opposition to virtually every U.S. position at the United Nations, and its activities within the nonaligned movement during those years further characterized India in American eyes as unfriendly to American interests. Consistent with this perception, beginning in the early 1970s every U.S. administration, including that of President Clinton, sought to erect higher and more robust policy, legal, and international regime obstacles between India and various strategic commodities so long as New Delhi persisted with its nuclear weapon programs. This was readily acknowledged by the under secretary of state for political affairs in the Clinton administration, Thomas Pickering, who, in the midst of warming U.S.-Indian relations, declared plainly that the "new and qualitatively closer relationship with India...cannot realize its full potential without further progress on nonproliferation," adding for good measure that "we also cannot and will not be able to concentrate on military issues until there is substantial progress on non-proliferation."[3]

What made NSSP an event of such significance in this context was that the Bush administration, exhibiting the same "revolutionary" oreign policy proclivities it has displayed in other areas, chose to turn Washington's long-standing approach to New Delhi on its head. Viewing India as part of the solution to nuclear proliferation rather than as part of the problem, President Bush embarked on a course of action that would permit India more—not less—access to controlled technologies even though New Delhi would not surrender its nuclear weapon program, refused to accede to the principal benchmarks laid down by the Clinton administration, and subsisted in its position formally outside the global nonproliferation regime. What the Bush administration asked for in return for this policy change was "merely" that India institutionalize comprehensive export controls that conformed to the best international standards and that New Delhi not use the technologies made available to it under NSSP to advance its own strategic weapon programs.

This change in approach derived from three evolving perceptions within the Bush administration. First, the administration had come to realize that India would not give up its nuclear weapons so long as various regional adversaries continued to possess comparable capabilities. The fact that the administration initially viewed both of India's antagonists—Pakistan and China—with considerable suspicion only made senior U.S. officials more sympathetic to New Delhi's predicament. *Second,* the administration was now of the understanding that India's nuclear weapons did not pose a threat to U.S. security and the United States' larger geopolitical interests, and could in certain circumstances actually advance American strategic objectives in Asia and beyond. The administration's own antipathy to nuclear arms control agreements such as the Comprehensive Test Ban Treaty and the Fissile Material Cut-off Treaty (which happened to dovetail with Indian interests on these issues), coupled with its strong expectation of an eventual renewal of great-power competition, allowed both realist and neoconservative factions within the administration to take a more relaxed view of New Delhi's emerging nuclear capabilities. *Third*, the administration now appreciated that the range of technological resources associated with weapons of mass destruction (WMD) and their delivery systems that were present in India in both the public and private sectors posed a far more serious threat to American safety—were these resources to be leaked, whether deliberately or inadvertently, to hostile regimes or nonstate actors—than New Delhi's ownership of various nuclear assets. These perceptions, which became dominant in administration thinking in regard to India post-9/11, made tightening the Indian export control regime far more important from the viewpoint of increasing U.S. security than leaning on the Indian state to cap or roll back its strategic programs. From these three perceptions grew the conviction that the United States ought to focus primarily on safeguarding India's tangible and intangible WMD capabilities, even as Washington struggled to find ways of accepting New Delhi's nuclear weaponry within the constraining framework of the existing international nonproliferation order.

Accordingly, the bargain encoded within NSSP affirmed that the United States would not let India's anomalous status within the global nonproliferation regime become an impediment to the close relationship desired by both sides. Toward that end, Washington would seek to build a partnership with New Delhi that included satisfying the latter's long-standing desire for greater access to restricted commodities in the areas of civilian nuclear energy, civilian space programs, dual-use high technology, and missile defense, so long as India did not seek to use these commodities to advance its own strategic programs or permit their unlawful export, nor countenanced the diffusion of its own advanced capabilities to any foreign entity. Because of the constraints imposed by U.S. law and the United States' existing commitments to various nonproliferation regimes, the kind of liberalization programmed into NSSP is inherently asymmetrical: Civilian nuclear energy remains the least developed aspect of the new partnership, with Washington, bound by prevailing restraints, able to demonstrate only modest forward movement, primarily in the area of nuclear safety. Where prior restraints have been weaker, for example, in the realms of civilian space cooperation, dual-use high technology, and missile defense, NSSP provides for more ambitious goals.

Although NSSP represented a political advance that bestowed material gains on both the United States and India, it nonetheless remained a *precarious* breakthrough from the viewpoint of radically transforming U.S.-Indian relations. For starters, the conviction among many of the principals in George W. Bush's first administration about the nonthreatening status—

and potential utility—of India's nuclear weapon programs did not permeate the bureaucracy as a whole. Even some senior officials, particularly in the State Department and Energy Department—rejecting larger divisions within the administration—were not entirely convinced, and this skepticism only gained in intensity at the middle and lower levels of government. Consequently, many officials interpreted NSSP in highly restrictive ways because of their continuing discomfort with both India's nuclear program and the administration's "exceptionalist" strategies for dealing with it.

Although NSSP represented a political advance, it nonetheless remained a precarious breakthrough from the viewpoint of radically transforming U.S.-Indian relations.

Further, NSSP itself reflected a degree of strategic hesitancy that is not surprising given the heated interagency debates that preceded its unveiling: In each of the four issue areas under its purview, the liberalization contemplated by the Bush administration extended only to policy change and not to amendments of domestic law or alterations in existing U.S. commitments to various international regimes. On many issues, the administration did not move as far as it could, even in the realm of policy shifts, because of concerns about the disruptive consequences for U.S. global antiproliferation activities arising from any effort to accommodate India.

Finally, despite embodying the administration's desire to craft a new approach to New Delhi, NSSP failed to provide a definitive answer to the question at the heart of any further transformation in U.S.-Indian relations: Is the prospective increase in Indian power beneficial or dangerous to the United States and its global interests? This uncertainty derived from fears that New Delhi was seeking to improve relations with Washington while simultaneously trying to avoid becoming locked in its embrace.

BEYOND NSSP: ADVANCING THE GROWTH OF INDIAN POWER

Uncertainties mattered little, however, in the early days of President Bush's .first term, when the administration singled out India as an emerging power with whom it sought a special relationship. U.S. ties with Pakistan and China—both threats to India—were at that time in varying states of disrepair. Today, however, this situation has been transformed on all counts. Although Washington's relationship with Islamabad is still oriented mainly toward avoiding a catastrophe arising from state failure (unlike the relationship with India, which is directed toward securing a greater good), Pakistan enjoys formal status as a Major Non-NATO Ally, and is an active collaborator in the U.S.-led action in Afghanistan, Operation Enduring Freedom, as well as a prominent beneficiary of U.S. economic assistance and the recipient of signi.- cant arms transfers from the United States.

China, too, has rapidly improved relations with the United States since the events of September 11, 2001. In contrast to the early months of President Bush's .first term, when China was routinely described as a "strategic competitor," administration policy now seeks a "confident, peaceful and prosperous China...as a global partner, able and willing to match its growing capabilities to its international responsibilities."[4]

The environment surrounding the ongoing transformation in U.S.-Indian relations is, thus, quite different today in comparison to what it was early in the .first term. While, as both sides acknowledge, U.S.-Indian relations are better than they have been since the Sino-Indian war of 1962, it is not yet obvious that this improving relationship can thrive—as it did in the heady days of 2001-2003—in the face of many competing pressures without concerted efforts by senior leaders in both Washington and New Delhi. The burdens on both sides today include the ongoing global war on terror, particularly the continuing challenges of stabilizing Iraq and Afghanistan (where U.S. and Indian interests converge, but are not entirely congruent); the renewed centrality of the U.S.- Pakistani relationship, including management of the consequences of major weapon sales to Islamabad and the threat of paralyzing India-Pakistan hyphenation in American bureaucratic habits; and the skepticism of many in the governing coalition in New Delhi—despite current prime minister Manmohan Singh's strong personal commitment to strengthened bilateral ties—about U.S. intentions and behavior both globally and in South Asia. Taken together, these encumbrances imply that if the United States is to completely fulfill the one unalloyed foreign policy achievement of President Bush's .first term—the transformation of U.S.-Indian relations—the administration will have to pay special attention to increasing the *substantive* gains that both sides, particularly India, enjoy as a result of their deepening ties.

Secretary of State Condoleezza Rice's March 16, 2005, visit to India (in the context of a larger trip to South Asia and East Asia) provided an opportunity to jump-start this process. Secretary Rice intimated the administration's intention when, replying to an Indian interlocutor's question on the significance of making New Delhi her .first stop, she said, "It really is emblematic of how far this relationship has come in the last several years. The President very much values the enhanced relationship between the United States and India, the fact that we are becoming in many ways important global partners as well as regional partners. And he wanted me very much to come here, and I'm glad that I was able to come here .first." Asserting that "we've tried very hard, as a matter of fact, to make the point that this is not a hyphenated relationship," Rice declared that U.S. ties with New Delhi ought to be viewed on their own terms: "This is a relationship with India. We also have a very good relationship with Pakistan and we are concerned about the well-being of both."[5]

These sentiments would be tested on Secretary Rice's return to Washington, when, after months of secret deliberation, President Bush .finally telephoned Prime Minister Singh, on March 25, 2005, to inform him personally that the United States would end the .fifteen-year hiatus in the sale of

F-16 .ghter aircraft to Pakistan. Singh, according to his spokesman, conveyed his "great disappointment at the decision, which could have negative consequences for India's security environment,"[6] but in a remarkable departure from the past, the Indian government's overall response was muted. This atypical reaction derived from the fact that even as the Bush administration was announcing prospective F-16 transfers to Pakistan, it unveiled a potentially far more radical initiative with respect to India. As three senior officials described it in a background briefing on the day of Bush's telephone call to Singh, the United States had in fact reached a decision "to help India become a major world power in the twenty-first century." By further asserting that "we understand fully the implications, including military implications, of that statement,"[7] the administration effectively gave notice that it would take to its limits the strategy advocated in an in-uential RAND report prior to Bush's election in 2000, namely, that the United States ought to "systemically decouple India and Pakistan [in its strategic calculations]: that is, U.S. relations with each state [should] be governed by an objective assessment of the intrinsic value of each country to U.S. interests rather than by fears about how U.S. relations with one would affect relations with the other."[8]

The widely noted sale of F-16s to Pakistan, and even more, the largely ignored commitment to advance India as a global power, thus represents a new U.S. strategy toward South Asia. It implicitly conveys to all within and beyond the region that the United States will do what it takes to help Pakistan transform itself into a successful and moderate state—including, as necessary, rewarding Pakistani president General Pervez Musharraf with military and economic assistance. But, more important, the United States will invest the energy and resources to enable India, the preeminent state in the region and an emerging success story internationally, to secure as untroubled an ascent to great-power status as possible through the instruments of U.S. support.

The widely noted sale of F-16s to Pakistan, and even more, the largely ignored commitment to advance India as a global power, thus represents a new U.S. strategy toward South Asia.

Toward that end, the Bush administration is pursuing two different kinds of initiatives simultaneously. First, it has decided—overcoming the hesitation of the past—to take a more liberal view in regard to supplying India with advanced defense systems. Accordingly, it has permitted Lockheed Martin and Boeing to offer F-16s and F-18s, respectively, as candidates for the Indian Air Force's multirole combat aircraft program, with the assurance that Washington would be favorably inclined to license even more sophisticated sensors and weapons than those made available to Pakistan and to consider coproduction of these platforms in India. The administration has also stated that it will support Indian requests for other "transformative systems in areas such as command and control, early warning and missile defense."9 Second, and even more important to India, the administration has decided to compress the schedule relating to NSSP implementation while expressing a willingness to discuss a range of contentious issues in three separate high-level dialogues with New Delhi: on strategic, energy, and economic concerns.

The strategic dialogue will focus on global security issues, including India's quest for permanent United Nations Security Council membership, future defense cooperation, high-technology trade, and space-related collaboration, as well as regional issues pertaining to security in and around South Asia. The energy dialogue will focus on energy security matters broadly understood, including the proposed Indian-Iranian-Pakistani gas pipeline, cooperation on nuclear safety, and, most important of all, ways of integrating India into the global nuclear regime so as to address New Delhi's desire for renewed access to safeguarded nuclear fuel and advanced nuclear reactors. The economic dialogue, which already exists in somewhat otiose form, will be resuscitated by high-level political and private-sector participation in order to increase U.S.-Indian economic interactions aimed at boosting India's growth and creating new constituencies in the United States with a stake in Indian power and prosperity.

On balance, therefore, the Bush administration's decision to expand relations with both its South Asian partners, but in a differentiated way commensurate with each state's geostrategic attractiveness to the United States, implies that Washington has placed its biggest bet on New Delhi, expecting that transformed bilateral relations will facilitate the expansion of Indian power in a manner that ultimately will advance America's own global interests with respect to defeating terrorism, arresting further nuclear proliferation, promoting democracy worldwide, and preserving a stable balance of power in Asia over the long term.

Thanks in part to heavy "backgrounding" by the Indian embassy in Washington and the Ministry of External Affairs in New Delhi, the response of Indian elites to this new Bush administration policy has generally been approving. Although several Indian commentators have expressed skepticism, reading the new approach as being little more than an effort to stoke Indian pride and obscure the "deeply unfriendly act"10 of selling F-16s to Pakistan, most analysts have had relatively positive reactions. Preferring to emphasize the gains accruing to India from Washington's latest policy turn, they have highlighted the administration's willingness to increase defense cooperation, including sale of major combat equipment; to revisit the issues of expanded civilian nuclear, space, and high-technology cooperation; and to accept India's emerging power as part of the "great changes in the world," which, as Secretary Rice noted when she was in New Delhi, "international institutions are going to have to start to accommodate ... in some way."11 Some commentators, however, drawing on Indian internal briefings, have gone much further, reading into various U.S. official remarks portents of imminent, dramatic policy changes. In one or two important instances, even the three sets of talks proposed by Rice as a way of strengthening U.S.-Indian relations were interpreted as implying the complete removal of all technology access controls imposed on India since its .first nuclear test in 1974.

Such an outcome is certainly possible—eventually. Indeed, progressively ending all technology restrictions pertaining to India ought to be the goal of the current transformation in U.S.-Indian relations. However, as things now stand, the three dialogues proposed by Secretary Rice represent innovations at the level of process, not breakthroughs at the level of outcomes. If these procedural advances are to become avenues through which major U.S. policy changes are to be implemented, both Washington and New Delhi will have to seize this opportunity boldly. The United States will have to ask itself whether it views India as a true partner in the exercise of its global management responsibilities and whether it would be willing to make the policy changes necessary in those issue areas important to New Delhi as a means of strengthening India's incentives to cooperate with Washington. India will have to ask itself whether it seeks to be relevant to those U.S. purposes that are ultimately its own as well, and whether it would be willing to shed its past inhibitions to work with the United States in some circumstances in which it may not have the luxury of hiding behind an existing international consensus. If both sides can answer these questions in the affirmative, the managerial improvements represented by the three dialogues could be transformed into potent mechanisms by which dramatic policy changes—which hitherto have eluded the Bush administration, even in NSSP—could be inaugurated, to the joint benefit of India and the United States.

These kinds of policy shifts, obviously, have not occurred as yet. But, they are what the Singh government is hoping for—and waiting to see before it decides how to respond to the U.S. decision to sell F-16s to Pakistan. No matter how unpalatable this sale is to Indian policy makers (and their private remarks corroborate their consternation abundantly), they have decided to overlook U.S.-assisted increases in Islamabad's military capability so long as such accretions are indeed marginal and so long as the Bush administration actually makes good on its intention to strengthen Indian power by adopting new policies on issues that are fundamentally important to New Delhi. Given this contingency underlying current Indian restraint, the administration ought to guard against complacency because the delicate balance within the Indian government, which at present makes for a muted response to Washington's defense sales to Islamabad, could quickly change into outright opposition if the United States were either to exceed certain qualitative or quantitative thresholds in its weapons transfers to Pakistan or to falter in its efforts to provide India with expanded access to various controlled technologies.

Successfully transforming the U.S.-Indian relationship, therefore, will require the Bush administration to pay careful attention both to the kinds of weapons transferred to Islamabad in the future and to the progress made in satisfying New Delhi's desire for critical technologies. The second is more important in any event, and grows intrinsically out of the administration's new national security objective of helping to advance the growth of Indian power. If this goal is to be attained, future U.S. policies will have to overcome the diffidence that kept revolutionary change from occurring in the areas of civilian nuclear, space, and high-technology cooperation within NSSP. This implies that the administration —if it is to meet Indian expectations in this regard—will not only have to push change to the limits permitted by current policy, but will have to change policy itself when necessary by working with Congress to seek the appropriate waivers from various legislative constraints (if amending the requisite laws is infeasible) and by coordinating with the international community to develop the appropriate carve-outs to enable treatment of New Delhi as a legitimate exception to the existing rules.

Before any of these activities are contemplated, however, President Bush ought to begin with an important initiative at the level of process. Given the complex, often bitter interagency wrangling that characterizes policy formulation and implementation within the U.S. government, and the proclivity of the bureaucracy to pursue its own interests irrespective of how these comport with political preferences, Bush should enshrine his intention to advance the growth of Indian power in a formal National Security Decision Directive (NSDD) that provides authoritative guidance for the entire government as it reviews various options that bear upon this issue. Absent such an instruction, it will be difficult to ensure that bureaucratic debates actually advance the president's interests. Besides serving as a statement that conveys both seriousness of purpose and clarity of intention, an NSDD provides an objective benchmark for judging different policy choices while ensuring that interagency decisions reflect presidential aims even when administration principals are not physically present to shape discussion.

In order to produce outcomes consistent with his desire "to help India become a major world power in the twenty-First century,"[12] President Bush should use the NSDD to direct that all levels of his administration adhere to this regulating principle:

Because of the unassailable congruence in bilateral objectives with respect to defeating terrorism, countering the spread of WMD, promoting democracy and economic development, and ensuring a stable balance of power in Asia, the fundamental strategic interests of the United States require

- strengthening India, supporting its democratic institutions, and assisting in the growth of its national power to satisfy both defense and developmental objectives
- integrating India as a friendly nuclear weapon state into the evolving global nuclear regime
- pursuing a special relationship with India that has as its goal maximizing the potential for strategic coordination such that, even though New Delhi continues to remain formally nonaligned, its foreign and security policies cohere more and more closely with those of the United States, and its national power is oriented toward achieving those joint gains of importance to both countries.

Enshrining these desiderata in the form of a new NSDD promulgated by the president—together with continuous high-level administration oversight—is essential if the three dialogues proposed by Secretary Rice are to drive major changes in U.S. policy that will, in her own words, "accelerate the relationship [and] take it to another level, if you will."[13]

INJECTING SUBSTANCE INTO PROCESS: AN AGENDA FOR ACTION

As a means of deepening their bilateral relationship, the United States and India are preparing to formally launch three new dialogues, pertaining to energy security, strategic cooperation, and economic engagement. These conversations should be initiated as soon as possible, with a view to having agreements on the most difficult policy issues in place and ready to be announced during the presidential visit to India scheduled for early 2006. Interim agreement on lesser matters ought to be announced along the way in order to bolster the momentum of the transforming relationship and to help immunize the Indian government against any domestic political opposition arising from future U.S. initiatives toward Pakistan. The dialogues proposed by Secretary Rice should be conducted at the highest possible levels, preferably by individuals who enjoy President Bush's personal condense. The agenda for these discussions is potentially so complex and contentious that any representation that does not meet these criteria will almost certainly assure either the irrelevance or the failure of the dialogues bureaucratically.

The Energy Dialogue

The creation of an energy dialogue as a means of jump-starting U.S.-Indian relations is both appropriate and urgent because insufficient access to energy remains one of the three great constraints on India's rapid economic growth and, by implication, its emergence as a great power. Unlike the problems posed by shortages of foreign investment and infrastructure weaknesses—the other two principal dampers on growth—the challenges related to energy cut across multiple realms—foreign policy, geopolitics, environmental concerns, and proliferation—and are not amenable to simple solutions that lie entirely, or even predominantly, within New Delhi's control. India's difficulties essentially arise from the fact that it is not well endowed with large primary energy reserves and has a poorly functioning energy market, yet must support a huge population and a large and rapidly modernizing economy. India is already the world's sixth-largest consumer of energy, and demand will likely more than double over the next quarter century, placing increased pressure on all sources: coal, oil, gas, hydroelectric power, and nuclear energy.

The biggest unilateral contribution India can make to address its energy problems is to develop pricing mechanisms that better reflect relative scarcity. Washington ought to press New Delhi on this issue through both the energy and the economic dialogues. The prospects for a sophisticated discussion on this subject are especially propitious because the U.S. delegation will be led by the secretary of energy, Samuel Bodman, a successful businessman with enormous experience in .- finance and industry. The Indian contingent will be led by the deputy chairman of the Planning Commission, the country's apex body responsible for determining growth and development priorities, assessing national resources, and formulating strategies for the effective and balanced utilization of these resources, Montek Singh Ahluwalia, who is one of India's most distinguished economists and a member of Manmohan Singh's original team of reformers, which oversaw the initial liberalization of the Indian economy in the early 1990s. Both delegations, therefore, will be led by senior officials who not only enjoy the confidence of their leaders but are sophisticated practitioners who understand the functioning of a modern market economy. The proposed structure of the energy dialogue itself, with its multiple working groups focused on oil and gas, electric power generation, clean coal, new energy sources, and nuclear power, permits a serious discussion about the value of introducing market mechanisms into all the core sectors of India's energy economy. Beyond restructuring the Indian energy market, however—which ought to be considered the .first order of business—the international community, and the United States in particular, can assist India by providing more liberal access to advanced technologies that increase the efficient use of existing energy sources, support conservation strategies, exploit new renewable energy reserves and nontraditional fuel concepts, and safely harness nuclear power.

The biggest unilateral contribution India can make to address its energy problems is to develop pricing mechanisms that better reflect relative scarcity.

While the energy dialogue ought to encompass all these issues in their entirety, three broad policy matters demand particular attention.

Focusing on Renewable Energy Technology

The United States remains a world leader in the development of renewable energy technologies. These technologies span a wide spectrum of sources, including biogas, biomass, solar energy, small hydropower plants, wind energy, ocean thermal energy, sea wave power, and tidal energy. Longer-term, though not strictly renewable, alternatives include opportunities associated with the hydrogen economy, a research and development area that has received concentrated attention in the United States and has also attracted interest in India. None of the sources of renewable energy, either singly or in combination, are panaceas for India's energy demands, given the problems of scale and the character of the technology involved. In many circumstances, they may be appropriate for Indian needs mainly on a micro or intermediate scale. However, because these solutions are technology intensive, the energy dialogue could play a critical role in creating institutional arrangements allowing American developers to interact with potential consumers of these specialized technologies in India. In most cases, the relevant technologies are highly sophisticated, but not controlled for any strategic reason. Consequently, developing mechanisms that increase information flows, offer .financing, and provide technical assistance represents an important avenue by which the United States could contribute to India's energy security in a sector that does not otherwise receive much attention. The energy discussions could also help to breathe new life into parleys on clean coal technologies, carbon sequestration, and the methaneto-markets concept, all of which were topics of conversation in the previous economic dialogue.

Managing Energy Geopolitics

India's large and rapidly growing demand for oil and natural gas will have to become one of the two major agenda items—the other being nuclear power—in any U.S.-Indian energy dialogue. While increasing access to American renewable energy technologies is important, such technologies will likely remain niche supplies of power for the foreseeable future. Oil and gas, in contrast, will continue to dominate strategic calculations, but the international energy market will for the most part regulate the resources available to India. An intergovernmental dialogue can best help indirectly, by increasing access to the myriad technologies that increase utilization and conservation efficiency in various industries (if these are controlled to begin with). It could also serve as a conduit for interactions between major U.S. energy suppliers and the government of India, particularly with respect to applying the Americans' high-technology assets to underwrite more effective prospecting in India's marginal or less accessible oil and gas fields. These benefits notwithstanding, the energy dialogue's real utility would lie in providing a forum where the intersection of energy and geopolitics could be discussed transparently. The United States has suggested the formation of a special steering committee to review all cross-cutting issues under the aegis of the energy dialogue's apex leadership. Under this eminently sensible proposal, the steering committee ought to be staffed by senior officials who are not only conversant with energy geopolitics but have ready access to their respective national leaderships, given the complicated subjects likely to come up for discussion in this body. In this context, the United States ought to begin the energy dialogue by committing itself to championing Indian membership in the International Energy Agency, since it makes little sense to exclude a major—and growing—energy consumer such as India from participating in this organization. Further, prospective transnational pipelines, issues on which the United States and India disagree, ought to receive high priority for discussion in the steering committee. Two such projects are particularly important: the Indian-Iranian-Pakistani and Burmese-Bangladeshi-Indian pipelines.

Although India enjoys good relations with Iran both geopolitically and economically, and has considered proposals for importing Iranian gas through pipelines for many years (as part of its larger energy security strategy), it has been a very reluctant player in the proposed Indian-Iranian-Pakistani pipeline. New Delhi's reservations here focus primarily on security: Fearing that a gas pipeline running through Pakistan might be vulnerable to cutoff in case of a crisis or war, India has taken the position that it does not want to be associated with the construction, maintenance, or operation of any energy transportation system running through Pakistani territory. Rather, New Delhi is of the view that Tehran would have to bear the costs (and the risks) of constructing an Iranian-Pakistani pipeline terminating at the India-Pakistan border—at which point India would be content to offered the gas under the terms of a purely bilateral Indian-Iranian agreement. In effect, the Indian "solution" would transform the Indian-Iranian-Pakistani pipeline into simply an Iranian-Pakistani conduit, with Iran responsible for compensating Pakistan through transit fees recovered from the price of gas exported to India.

As far as the United States is concerned, therefore, New Delhi is in effect telling Washington that India remains simply another consumer of Iranian energy and that all U.S. complaints about the pipeline ought to be directed at the United States' ally, Pakistan. India is and will continue to be a consumer of Iranian gas—as are many other states, including important U.S. allies such as Japan—but the politics of the pipeline remain a matter for discussion between Tehran and Islamabad. Even if these negotiations are successful, the two bilateral pacts necessary to make the solution work—an Iranian-Indian accord on gas, and an Iranian-Pakistani agreement on the pipeline—are far from being done deals. India has taken the position that any price above the US$3 per million British thermal units (BTUs) currently being paid by its power and fertilizer sectors for gas on the international market is unacceptable. Iran, in contrast, appears to be seeking more than US$4 per million BTUs, a rate that will only go higher if Pakistani transit fees are added.

U.S. concerns about these pipeline-related transactions obviously have less to do with cost than with the United States' desire to enforce the isolation of Iran and deny it increased energy revenues resulting from expanded exports to India. While the Bush administration's position is consistent with its overall policy, Washington has multiple reasons not to involve itself in the arrangement among India, Iran, and Pakistan, whatever its .final form. To begin with, India will continue to import Iranian gas to meet its growing energy needs, whether such imports are delivered in seaborne containers or through an overland pipeline. The United States has not attempted to obstruct either ongoing Group of Eight energy investments in Iran or past Indian-Iranian energy trade, so singling out this extension of existing activity under the Iran-Libya Sanctions Act on the grounds that it advances Iran's capacity to engage in pernicious behaviors is counterproductive: It introduces unnecessary irritants into the relationship with India, even as it fails to prevent gas exports that would occur anyway (albeit less efficiently), by sea.

Pakistan, an important American ally, actually stands to benefit economically from an Indian-Iranian-Pakistani arrangement (even if the same consists only of separate bilateral deals). Facilitating Pakistan's economic growth contributes to the larger U.S. strategic objectives of transforming Pakistan into a moderate state and increasing Pakistani solvency, the latter being one reason why Islamabad is the biggest champion of the pipeline. Increased economic interdependence between India and Pakistan, even if achieved only circuitously through separate bilateral arrangements, can be an important confidence-building measure. More important, it would help develop patterns of stable cooperation that could advance the peace process in South Asia—a regional objective that is also of great importance to the United States.

Finally, assent to the Indian-Iranian-Pakistani gas transit arrangement could become another positive incentive for the United States to offer Tehran to forsake its nuclear weapon ambitions. The Bush administration has already made the policy decision to support the United Kingdom, France, and Germany in encouraging Iran to end its enrichment program permanently by offering incentives in principle; there is good reason, given all the other American interests in South Asia, to add a waiver of the Iran-Libya Sanctions Act as it pertains to any pipeline to the set of inducements Washington can offer Tehran in exchange for good behavior on the nuclear question.

A similar set of considerations ought to apply to the prospective Burmese-Bangladeshi-Indian pipeline. Washington's dislike of the military leadership in Myanmar (Burma) has resulted in a difference of opinion with New Delhi on the latter's efforts to engage Yangon. Indian policy makers are under no illusions about the odious nature of the State Peace and Development Council (SPDC), the Burmese junta formerly known as the State Law and Order Restoration Council (SLORC), which has been in power since 1988. For many years—consistent with U.S. policy—New Delhi shunned the SPDC in favor of strong support for the democratic opposition led by Aung San Suu Kyi. Only when New Delhi realized that the Chinese were exploiting the SPDC's international isolation to make geopolitical inroads into Myanmar did India turn around and attempt to engage the military regime. To this day, New Delhi remains confected about this policy: Like Washington, it would prefer to isolate the Burmese dictatorship if that would contribute to its downfall. Since this outcome is judged unlikely—even by the United States—India is faced with the challenge of coping with Chinese penetration of Myanmar even as the SPDC continues to tighten its hold on power.

India views the future Burmese-Bangladeshi-Indian pipeline as a constrained choice that, luckily, addresses multiple problems simultaneously: It provides a means of weaning the SPDC away from excessive dependence on China, and thereby limits Beijing's penetration along a frontier of great strategic importance to India; it represents another avenue for mitigating India's own acute energy shortages; and it affords Bangladesh an opportunity to bring its substantial but as-yet untapped gas reserves to market in a remunerative way. The high capital costs of the planned pipeline and the Bangladeshi government's paranoia about natural resource exports (a legacy of Pakistan's exploitative internal colonialism prior to the civil war that gave birth to Bangladesh in 1971) represent the two most acute near-term challenges to bringing the project to fruition. Given U.S. interest in helping secure India's energy supply, fostering the economic development of Bangladesh itself (among other reasons, to counter the rising Islamist tide in the country), and arresting the growth of Chinese influence in the Indian Ocean rimlands, Washington at least ought to stay its opposition, if it cannot bring itself to support the pipeline.

Assisting India with Civilian Nuclear Power

The energy dialogue represents the best means of reaching a U.S.-Indian modus vivendi on civilian nuclear power. Given its huge energy requirements, the growing pressures to avoid burning dirty coal in order to protect the environment, and the need to reduce carbon emissions that exacerbate global warming, New Delhi has little alternative but to rely increasingly on nuclear power. Unfortunately for India, two major challenges threaten this objective.

Most fundamentally, India's anomalous existence as a nuclear weapon power not recognized under the Nuclear Non-Proliferation Treaty (NPT) has cast it into a nether world where it is denied the right to engage in the open technical and commercial collaboration on the peaceful uses of nuclear energy available to all other legitimate nuclear weapon states. India, in fact, has been among the chief targets of a worldwide technology denial regime intended to prevent states from acquiring various capabilities relating to the production of both nuclear power and nuclear weaponry. Given these constraints, India has developed a substantial indigenous capability on both counts over the years, but even these are insufficiently to meet its national needs. Where nuclear power is concerned, questions about the safety of indigenous reactors continue to dog the Indian Department of Atomic Energy. And the country's vast future electricity demands imply that India will require advanced nuclear power plants with much higher unit outputs than can be secured merely through the scaling up of existing designs. In other words, India will need many new, large, reliable reactors that will meet the safety standards taken for granted in developed societies, together with all the advanced waste management systems required to keep the nuclear fuel cycle as a viable source of energy for the Indian economy.

Equally relevant is the fact that despite its great size, India has the misfortune to have been poorly endowed with natural uranium. It has been estimated that these modest reserves of about 70,000 metric tons will suffice to produce no more than approximately 10 gigawatts of electric power, if used in the pressurized heavy water reactors (PHWRs) currently operating or under construction. India's natural uranium deficiency has resulted in a commitment to an ambitious, technically challenging three-stage program designed to exploit the country's thorium reserves, which at an estimated 290,000 metric tons remain the second largest in the world. In stage 1 of this program, a series of indigenously constructed PHWRs fueled by scarce natural uranium have been used since the late 1960s to generate electricity and produce plutonium as a by-product. The focus of stage 2 is on constructing fast neutron reactors that will burn the plutonium produced in the stage 1 PHWRs in order to breed a uranium isotope, U-233, from the thorium blanket surrounding the plutonium in the fuel pellet. A major step toward stage 2 capability was taken when the 13-megawatt (electric) fast breeder test reactor (FBTR) at Kalpakkam, which uses uranium-plutonium carbide fuel, attained criticality in 1985. Another milestone was reached in 1997, when electricity from the Kalpakkam FBTR .owed into the southern Indian power grid. This achievement notwithstanding, India still does not have any fast breeder reactors operating on a commercial scale. This implies that the country is still short of the requisite quantities of U-233 required for achieving energy independence in the manner envisaged in the three-stage plan; consequently, the 420 gigawatts (electric) power potential believed to exist in stage 2 of the program remains more or less notional today. Stage 3, which is many decades away, will involve construction of advanced heavy water reactors (AHWRs) that will use the U-233 produced in stage 2, encased in a thorium blanket, to generate about two-thirds of these reactors' output from the thorium casing itself. Since fast neutron reactors are designed to produce more U-233 than they consume, and since India has enormous reserves of thorium, the stage 3 facilities currently being planned could in principle produce 358,000 gigawatts (electric) of power annually, sufficient to meet the country's energy requirements during this century and beyond.

The problems with this grandiose scheme, however, are as much economic as they are technical. Creating the infrastructure to enable New Delhi to produce electricity in this fashion involves enormous capital outlays, and it is by no means clear that India has mastered either the technical challenges involved in separating U-233 on a commercial scale or the waste management issues associated with this process to an extent sufficient to guarantee the success of the three-stage master plan. Problems here include the high cost and technical complications of fuel fabrication due partly to the high radioactivity of U-233, which is invariably contaminated with traces of U-232; the difficulties of recycling thorium due to the presence of highly radioactive Th-228; and the various technical risks associated with reprocessing in thorium-based fuel cycles, which have not yet been satisfactorily resolved. Not surprisingly, then, even the World Nuclear Association, an industry group dedicated to the promotion of nuclear energy, was compelled to conclude that "much development work is still required before the thorium fuel cycle can be commercialized, and the effort required seems unlikely while (or where) abundant uranium is available."[14]

While the difficulties of mastering the thorium-based fuel cycle will preoccupy India for many years to come, New Delhi is confronted by more pressing threats. The critical problem facing India right now is the severe shortage of natural uranium, which, if unresolved, could bring the operation of many stage 1 PHWRs to a gradual halt. Not only would this worsen India's electricity production problems—with all the consequent implications for economic growth—but it would also decisively undermine the three-stage program on which the Department of Atomic Energy has staked the nation's energy independence for the secular future.

Therefore, if India can be assured stable supplies of natural uranium over the long term, it is possible that national decision makers will not feel compelled to invest in the more risky stage 2 component of its nuclear energy program on any but an experimental scale. Alternatively, if India is provided unconstrained access to various types of advanced reactors together with their appropriate fuels, it is likely that New Delhi will postpone implementation of the three-stage cycle, a program that would, incidentally, leave the country awash with more plutonium than it could ever use either for energy production or nuclear weaponry. Under the current nonproliferation regime, India can secure both fuel and reactors only on condition that it roll back its nuclear weapon program and adopt full-scope safeguards, which would mean making *all* current and future nuclear facilities subject to International Atomic Energy Agency (IAEA) inspection. Since India is unlikely to accept such obligations—having resisted them for many decades—the challenge for the international community, and for the United States in particular, in the context of the energy dialogue, will be to craft a solution that allows New Delhi access to peaceful nuclear technology even while it retains its nuclear weapons. Integrating India into the global nuclear regime in this fashion will be a burdensome task, but the alternative implies that New Delhi will be condemned to pursue autarkic nuclear energy production strategies that are technically hazardous, pose potential threats to public safety and the environment, and involve producing huge stocks of weapon-usable plutonium.

It is unlikely that the United States and India will be able in the near term to find a completely satisfying solution to the conundrum of providing New Delhi access to safeguarded nuclear fuel and technology while allowing India to keep its nuclear weaponry. Even if the U.S. domestic constraints on such access, encoded in the Atomic Energy Act of 1954 (as amended) and the 1978 Nuclear Non-Proliferation Act, can be eased by presidential waivers supported by Congress, the larger question remains of how the United States can treat India as an exception to the international nonproliferation order without undermining that regime in the process. The fundamental issue here is not one of either law or precedent, both of which can be altered if a consensus in support of such action can be created. Rather, the challenge is essentially structural, revolving around how the United States can bestow a special nuclear status on India without opening the door to other countries that might be tempted to demand comparable indulgence. Since all non–nuclear weapon states currently enjoy access to safeguarded nuclear fuel and technology only if they have renounced their right to nuclear weaponry, treating India as the exception could unravel the entire nonproliferation regime at a time when it is already under threat from multiple sources and when a stronger nonproliferation system is viewed as critical to U.S. national security.

Resolving this problem will be neither rapid nor easy. Many of the expectations currently voiced in India—for instance, that the United States can settle this issue in simple bilateral fashion or through straightforward unilateral action—are entirely misplaced. While Washington ought to look for ways to satisfy New Delhi's need for nuclear energy, any discussion about integrating India into the global nonproliferation order writ large is likely to be extraordinarily difficult, as scrutiny of the following .five illustrative options—listed in order of increasing difficulty—will suggest:

1. inviting India to participate in international research and development efforts pertaining to peaceful uses of nuclear energy
2. offering India access to nuclear safety technologies for its reactors
3. supplying India with various items for use within the steam

cycle in safeguarded reactors

4. permitting India to purchase safeguarded nuclear fuel from the international market

5. permitting India to purchase nuclear technology (including nuclear reactors) from Nuclear Suppliers Group (NSG) members or directly from U.S. suppliers

The simplest initiative the United States could undertake to satisfy New Delhi's need for civilian nuclear technology, even if only partially, would be to invite India to participate in international research efforts pertaining to the development of advanced nuclear reactors. The three most important initiatives in this regard are Generation IV, ITER, and the Radkowsky Thorium Fuel (RTF) program. Generation IV consists of ten countries working together under the aegis of the U.S. Department of Energy's Office of Nuclear Energy, Science, and Technology to examine concepts that could lead to future reactor designs that are economical, safe, proliferation resistant, and minimally waste producing. ITER (formerly the International Thermonuclear Experimental Reactor) involves six countries experimenting under the auspices of the IAEA with a hydrogen plasma torus, the goal being to design and build the nuclear fusion power plants needed to meet tomorrow's energy needs. The RTF program, directed by the Brookhaven National Laboratory in collaboration with an international team that includes several Russian research institutes, the Massachusetts Institute of Technology, and Ben Gurion University in Israel, aims to develop proliferation-resistant nuclear fuel cycles using thorium, India's naturally plentiful radioactive element. India has already expressed great interest in participating in all three projects. Given the enormous demands that will be made on nuclear power in India in the decades ahead, the United States could provide major assistance in developing safe, efficient, proliferationresistant next-generation reactors by permitting India to participate in these ongoing research and experimental activities.

If the administration wanted to meaningfully enhance civilian nuclear cooperation with India, inviting New Delhi into nuclear research and development activities represents the least controversial option.

Of the many challenges to bilateral cooperation in the nuclear arena generally, those impeding India's integration into research endeavors would be easier to overcome than most. The Atomic Energy Act permits the U.S. Department of Energy to authorize any entity to engage directly or indirectly in the production of special nuclear materials upon a determination by the secretary of energy that such activity will not undermine the interests of the United States. Employing Section 57 of the Act, which would permit institutions or individuals to provide India with technical advice, training, and consultation, the Bush administration could permit India to join the Generation IV, ITER, and RTF programs. The United States has hitherto avoided soliciting Indian participation because it has sought to scrupulously uphold the core nonproliferation principle animating the NSG, which affirms that any access to civilian nuclear technology—either tangible or intangible—by a non–nuclear weapon state requires acceptance of full-scope safeguards. Admitting India to research efforts such as Generation IV, ITER, and RTF would therefore be in connect with the prohibition against intangible transfers that is currently encoded in the laws, nonproliferation policy, and international regime commitments of the United States.

Yet if the Bush administration wanted to meaningfully enhance civilian nuclear cooperation with India while simultaneously minimizing damage to the existing nuclear regime, inviting New Delhi into these research and development activities represents the least controversial option. For starters, it involves no physical conveyance of technology; further, the prohibition against intangible transfers arguably ought not to apply in this case since the research programs of interest are focused primarily on the discovery of *prospective* knowledge. Since such knowledge by definition does not yet exist, a proscription on its transfer risks being meaningless. Consequently, at least as far as India is concerned, the standing injunctions against intangible transfers ought not be used as impediments to New Delhi's participation in such nuclear research programs. Admittedly, all these justifications would be controversial; further, they underscore the likelihood that any effort to integrate India into civilian nuclear energy research and development programs will require a strong presidential commitment to making important policy changes that move the United States away from its currently rigid prohibitions against intangible transfers, as well as a willingness to pursue the relevant consultations within the NSG to minimize erosion of the international nonproliferation regime.

In summary, Indian partnership in global civilian nuclear energy research programs is a relatively achievable objective, given that it would fall substantially within the domain of presidential initiative. Moreover, as successive U.S. Nuclear Regulatory Commission (NRC) chairmen who have visited India have come to appreciate, Indian nuclear science could actually contribute to the success of these research efforts, thanks, paradoxically, to the enormous repository of indigenous theoretical and engineering capability that has been developed as a result of decades of forced isolation.

The first alternative, therefore, represents an easier, though not entirely trouble-free, choice. The second option for integrating India into the nonproliferation order, offering access to reactor safety technologies, would be trickier than simply inviting participation in research and development programs because it would mean granting more intimate access to the technology used in nuclear reactors. Through NSSP, the United States tentatively began offering India expanded access to safety equipment, but only for its four safeguarded reactors (of the fourteen currently in operation and nine under construction). While current U.S. policy represents an improvement over that prior to NSSP, it is still insufficiently. The safety technologies presently on offer for India's safeguarded plants are for the most part trivial and well within New Delhi's capacity to produce or procure indigenously. Further, they are mostly external monitoring devices that do nothing to enable India to operate its reactors more safely. Such dubious generosity risks trivializing the notion of safety cooperation, and makes no difference whatsoever to the safety of even the few safeguarded facilities qualified in principle to enjoy access to controlled technologies. Part of the difficulty, however, is technical: A nuclear reactor is a complex "system of systems," in which every component makes some contribution to safe operation. By this yardstick, meaningful safety cooperation would require that India receive access to the entire range of reactor components, from pressure vessels, control rods, coolant pumps, and pressure tubes to heat exchangers and instrumentation. Adopting this approach would violate both the domestic law and the international obligations of the United States, not to mention rendering absurd the notion of *safety* cooperation.

Even if this problem can be resolved through some technical consensus about what contributes directly—and solely—to plant safety, highly restrictive U.S. domestic and international obligations would make for excessively conservative policies that provide no substantive palliatives to the quandaries of reactor safety. In its recent report, *Universal Compliance: A Strategy for Nuclear Security*, the Carnegie Endowment recommended, albeit with caveats, that "the Nuclear Suppliers Group should remove restrictions on transferring equipment that these states [meaning India, Pakistan, and Israel] need in order to bring safeguarded nuclear plants up to the highest safety standards. This should include 'trigger list' technology if necessary."[15] This eminently sensible suggestion ought to be adopted by the United States vis-à-vis

India, but the difficulties inherent in doing so should not be underestimated. For example, it would require that the U.S. government make available commodities that are controlled under part 1 of the NSG Guidelines and that are licensed by the NRC in the United States. The best candidates here for liberalized access remain in-core and ex-core neutron detection and measuring instruments, which are used to determine neutron .ux levels within or outside the reactor vessel and as a result directly contribute to its safe operation. Washington would also have to open the door to a range of safety-related dualuse technologies regulated by the Department of Commerce (and whose use is consistent with part 2 of the NSG Guidelines) that are currently controlled under the "NP 1" and "NP 2" designations in U.S. Export Administration Regulations. Technologies in the NP 2 category, such as generators and other equipment specially designed, prepared, or intended for use with nuclear plants, and special piping, .fittings, and valves made of special alloys for nuclear plants, can be released relatively easily because they are unilaterally controlled by the United States. Affording India more liberal access to safety-related NP 1 technologies, such as radiation-shielding windows, radiation-hardened cameras, radiation-hardened robots, and the myriad instrumentation devices categorized as dualuse items having nuclear applications, is much more problematic. These items are subject to NSG guidelines that presuppose full-scope safeguards, but the U.S. government can still permit, albeit more uncomfortably, their transfer to safeguarded Indian reactors. Three conditions must be met, however: that the equipment remain under IAEA safeguards, that it not be used to support research or development relating to any nuclear explosive device, and that it not be retransferred without the prior consent of the United States.

Where safeguarded reactors are concerned, therefore, the U.S. president can expand India's access to safety-related technologies with varying degrees of difficulty: Dual-use technologies categorized as NP 2, and peripheral items in the EAR-99 group, which represent items subject to the export licensing jurisdiction of the Department of Commerce but do not possess explicit Export Control Classification Numbers (ECCN) on the Commerce Control List (CCL), can be transferred easily; dual-use technologies categorized as NP 1 can also be offered, but with much greater difficulty, because doing so would require coordination with various NSG partners; providing "trigger list" items would be the most controversial because it would require the consent of Congress and the NRC, coordination with the NSG, and invocation of the "exceptional circumstances" principle regulating transfers intended to prevent a radiological hazard.

Assisting India with respect to enhancing nuclear safety involves more than simply providing New Delhi with various technologies: As the Indian Department of Atomic Energy has repeatedly averred, the knowledge gained from the safe operation of U.S. nuclear facilities could often be more valuable to India than the mere transfer of some discrete gadgets or components. Over the years, Indian atomic energy officials have repeatedly sought information about technical safety practices, plant aging data, operational safety procedures, .re safety, probabilistic safety assessments, benchmark analyses utilizing standard problems, and emergency operating procedures—often without much success. Sharing some of this information could put India and the United States afoul of the standing prohibitions against intangible transfers, but much of it can be offered to India without prejudice. In any event, all such initiatives would uniformly require substantial changes in Bush administration policies and would, as such, remain suitable subjects for the energy dialogue.

Even if significant transfers of safety-related information and technology were to occur, however, most Indian nuclear reactors—being unsafeguarded —would continue to lie outside the ambit of such U.S. assistance. This prospect raises the specter of reactor accidents, which cannot be addressed because U.S. domestic law and international agreements combine to treat unsafeguarded reactors as beyond the pale of policy reform. Since accidents at these facilities could be equally devastating to ordinary Indians and to populations beyond India's borders, the Bush administration ought to give serious thought to structural solutions that go beyond the expansion of safety cooperation to the small number of safeguarded reactors. The outlines of a possible solution are discussed in the sub-section following, but here it suffices to say that because India is unlikely to be willing to put all its reactors under safeguards merely to secure safety technologies, the United States is actually faced with the much larger challenge of devising a strategy that integrates New Delhi into the evolving global nuclear order without disturbing it more than is necessary.

The third option, which would deepen U.S.- Indian cooperation in the realm of civilian nuclear energy, would be to provide India with various items restricted to the steam cycle in present and future safeguarded Indian reactors. In the discussions leading up to NSSP, a variant of this option received serious consideration from the United States but was ultimately rejected because of the strong objections of the State Department's Non-Proliferation Bureau, which adopted a highly conservative reading of the presumed impact on U.S. nonproliferation policy globally.

The Bush administration ought to review this decision and at the very least support the sale to New Delhi of all *dual-use* "balance of plant" components —listed in part 2 of the NSG Guidelines and controlled by the NRC and Department of Commerce through the Nuclear Referral List—because these items would be comparable to those available to any Indian power plant that did not use controlled nuclear .ssion to produce steam. Given the design of India's CANDU reactors, separating steam cycle components from explicitly nuclear subsystems—calendria, fuel, fueling machines, moderators, and internals—is easier than in many other kinds of reactors. Ideally, making such a distinction would lead to a policy of permitting India to purchase *all* steam cycle components, including those on the trigger list, such as heat exchangers. Since these are controlled exclusively by the NRC, consistent with part 1 of the NSG Guidelines, they cannot be made available to India under current policy.

The administration therefore ought to consider whether it would be willing to transfer such technologies to all Indian nuclear reactors, current and future, were they to be placed under international safeguards. Under such a regime, only the specifically nuclear components of a reactor—meaning the reactor vessel, fuel machines, control rods and equipment, pressure tubes, primary coolant pumps, and reactor internals—would lie beyond New Delhi's reach. All other components would be available to any Indian reactor that was subject to IAEA inspections. Whether this solution would be acceptable to India is difficult to say because it has never been discussed with New Delhi, but a policy that bestowed genuine access to *all* steam cycle components could tempt India to place many, if not all, its power reactors under safeguards. In the interim, there is a strong case to be made for permitting at least the sale of all dualuse steam cycle components for New Delhi's current and future safeguarded nuclear reactors as a partial solution until the larger problems related to India's integration into the global nuclear order are sorted out. As is the case with the second option (providing access to safety technology), this is a decision that lies within the purview of the executive branch but would require the acquiescence of the NRC and Congress as well as consultations with the NSG.

The fourth and .fifth options—respectively, permitting India to purchase safeguarded nuclear fuel on the international market and letting India acquire nuclear reactors and other nuclear technology from NSG members or directly from U.S. suppliers—represent the most ambitious alternatives that could be considered in the energy dialogue. Both would be extremely difficult choices because current U.S. law and international regime obligations permit such transactions only with legitimate nuclear weapon states (defined as states that detonated a nuclear device prior to 1967) or with non-nuclear states that accept full-scope safeguards. Since India falls into neither category, and seems unlikely to accept comprehensive safeguards in the immediate future, Washington will be unable to satisfy New Delhi's desire for stable supplies of nuclear fuel and imported nuclear reactors without .finding a way to formally integrate India into the existing nonproliferation order.

The U.S.-built nuclear reactor at Tarapur, however, provides a small, but important, opportunity to address the problem of fuel supply at least insofar as this facility is concerned. The Tarapur reactor was constructed and remains operational under safeguards. Being a boiling water reactor, it requires low-enriched uranium for its operation —a fuel that India has had to import repeatedly from multiple suppliers under the "exceptional circumstances" clause of the NSG Guidelines because the United States reneged on its contractual obligation to provide fuel thanks to a retrospective application of the Nuclear Nonproliferation Act of 1978. Given this history, the Tarapur facility provides an opportunity for the United States to demonstrate its willingness to help India resolve its nuclear fuel problems in at least this one instance in any of three different ways: (1) the United States could resume supplying safeguarded fuel under the safety principle in domestic and international regulations; (2) it could permit other NSG members or other states to supply India with the fuel in a manner consistent with safeguards under the same safety doctrine; (3) it could help India to fuel the reactor with indigenously produced mixed oxide fuel by providing the technologies required to modify the calendria for this purpose. Bringing closure to the vexed problem of Tarapur, whose output is vital to the electricity consumers of the city of Bombay, would be a splendid token of U.S. support for India's efforts to meet its energy challenges.

All solutions that involve granting India routine access to imported nuclear fuel and reactors (or even "one-time" rights to exceptionally large quantities of natural uranium sufficient to power India's PHWRs over their lifetimes) will require structural adjustments to the global nonproliferation regime. This may even be the case for many lower-end alternatives as well, such as involving India in research and development toward peaceful uses of nuclear energy and offering access to reactor safety technology, if the Bush administration is to avoid a pattern of ad hoc or furtive decisions favoring New Delhi.

Integrating India into the Global Nuclear Regime

Where integrating India into the international nonproliferation order is concerned, six end-states can be imagined:

1. The status quo survives with India continuing in its state of isolation with no access to safeguarded nuclear fuel and technology.

2. India is permitted access to safeguarded nuclear fuel and technology in exchange for bringing all its present and future nuclear reactors under safeguards and completely terminating .fissile material production (but with the right

to retain, without accounting, existing stocks of .fissile material or weapons, or both).

3. India is permitted access to safeguarded nuclear fuel and technology in exchange for bringing all its present and future nuclear reactors under safeguards (but with the right to retain, without accounting, existing stocks of .fissile material or weapons, or both, while continuing with the production of .fissile materials under safeguards).

4. India is permitted access to safeguarded nuclear fuel and technology in exchange for bringing all its present and future power reactors under safeguards (but with no constraints on its ability to continue producing unsafeguarded .fissile materials by means of its two research reactors).

5. India is permitted access to safeguarded nuclear fuel and technology in exchange for bringing all its present and future power reactors under safeguards (but with no constraints on its ability either to continue producing unsafeguarded .fissile materials by means of its two research reactors or to upgrade or increase the number of research reactors dedicated to producing unsafeguarded weaponsgrade .fissile materials).

6. India is formally integrated into the NPT regime as a legitimate nuclear weapon state, with all the privileges thereof.

Elements of the American nonproliferation community both inside and outside the U.S. government, as well as nonproliferation constituencies abroad, adamantly argue in favor of the .first outcome, maintenance of the status quo, for a variety of reasons, some focused on penalizing India for its resistance to the global nonproliferation order and others on what integrating India under various conditions might mean for the future success of that order. All those entities dened by a singular passion for nonproliferation usually end up supporting this alternative. Other, more reform-minded groups, which take into account both the reality of India's nuclear weapons (whether they like them or not) and the necessity of enmeshing India in the global nuclear order, settle for some variant of the nuclear access envisioned in the second and third end-states. This position is defended prima facie on the grounds that it would accommodate Indian security interests (in that New Delhi would get to keep its nuclear weapons and its previously produced .fissile materials without accounting) while permitting the United States to defend India's inclusion in the nuclear trading community because India would have effectively brought all its nuclear facilities *post factum* under full-scope safeguards, and hence would be deserving of the privileges accorded to all NPT signatories in good standing.

While there is much to commend in the reformist argument, it still takes its bearings predominantly from nonproliferation concerns and not from the competing but equally vital issues related to the balance of power in Asia and beyond. By integrating India into the nonproliferation order at the cost of capping the size of its eventual nuclear deterrent, the second solution, and perhaps the third, threaten to place New Delhi at a severe disadvantage vis-à-vis Beijing, a situation that could not only undermine Indian security but also U.S. interests in Asia in the face of the prospective rise of Chinese power over the long term. These options too are unlikely to appeal to India at this time, because New Delhi currently possesses only a relatively small stockpile of weapons-grade .fissile materials. Consequently, they should emphatically not be endorsed by the Bush administration in the energy dialogue because they advance one important near-term U.S. objective—integrating India into the nonproliferation order—at the cost of the longer-term and perhaps more important goal of assuring a stable balance of power in Asia. So long as this latter objective remains critical to the United States, the administration ought to expend its energies on devising ways to implement either the fourth or the .fifth option, either of which, in placing fewer constraints on India than the .first three alternatives, is more consistent with the regulating principle that underlies the NSDD recommended earlier in the present work (under the heading "Beyond NSSP: Advancing the Growth of Indian Power"). In this context, the United States ought to forgo pursuing the sixth alternative—India's formal integration into the NPT regime—because

It would be not only far too difficult but unnecessary, given that the fourth and .fifth alternatives would bestow on India all the benefits conferred by formal NPT membership except status. It would be hard to overstate the difficulty of integrating India into the global nuclear order through either of the preferred options. At the moment it is not at all obvious, rhetoric in the Indian press notwithstanding, that the Bush administration has the intent, the resolve, or the capacity to press these initiatives, given the immense burdens they would impose on the United States. Yet option four or .five is precisely what should be pursued if the administration is serious about transforming its relations with India. Unfortunately, either option would advance goals that collide most directly with the same universal regimes the United States has assiduously sought to sustain over the last several decades. Consequently, it is obvious that the administration will be unable to make good on its new commitment to further Indian power without confronting this contradiction directly.

Why the United States ought to assist India at the risk of undermining the global nonproliferation regime becomes, then, the central question facing U.S. policy makers. In the .first instance, Washington ought to support New Delhi simply because its presence outside the global nonproliferation architecture will be increasingly dangerous for U.S. interests, given India's vast and growing indigenous capabilities. Although the Indian government has good incentives of its own to institute rigorous export controls—and its record in regard to nuclear proliferation is exemplary despite its exclusion from the international regime—there is no assurance that these restraints will be consistently or effectively enforced in perpetuity if for any reason New Delhi is confronted with burdensome direct costs as a result. Preventing outward proliferation is in many ways a public good where the potential disparity between possibly high direct costs in the near term and the translucent indirect benefits over the long term to a given state often results in effective implementation of export controls being under-produced. The temptation to violate nonproliferation norms, as shown most recently in Pakistan, derives ultimately from these inequalities between private and collective costs and benefits. There is therefore a non-trivial risk that, absent consequential material inducements, Indian enforcement of export controls over the long term could fall short of the performance level necessary to prevent the materialization of serious threats to U.S. interests. Encouraging the government of India to enact strong export control legislation, as is current U.S. policy, engages but does not resolve the core question of why New Delhi would want to enforce such regulations consistently—over the long haul—if there were no larger payoff in terms of direct material benefits specifically accruing to India.

As neoclassical economic theory has convincingly demonstrated, producing adequate levels of public goods involves overcoming vexing problems of collective action. Often this requires that "privileged" agents provide "supernormal" subsidies to all other entities involved in the resolution of these dilemmas, meaning thereby that those who would be most affected by the nonproduction of any specific public good usually have to contribute disproportionately in order to overcome its customary deficit. Providing India with access to safeguarded nuclear fuel and technology represents one form of supernormal subsidy. The international nonproliferation regime already provides such benefits to *all* its members in that legitimate nuclear and non–nuclear weapon states in good standing are guaranteed access to the peaceful uses of nuclear energy. Of the three outliers, Pakistan and Israel receive their subsidies in different form, namely, through large aid programs and privileged political relations with the United States. Only

India is currently situated outside the circle of such subvention, yet it is expected to contribute just the same toward the realization of global nonproliferation goals. Beyond a certain point, virtue cannot remain its own reward—so long as the international system is populated by pervasively egoistic yet rational utility-maximizing entities. Given that reality, the United States ought to increase India's access to civilian nuclear energy in an ordered way that implies integration with the global regime, because this course of action alone provides the best guarantee that New Delhi will scrupulously control its national capabilities permanently and thus choke off the only real security threat emanating from India to the United States.

In the final analysis, however, accommodating India on the issue of nuclear cooperation is desirable because it is fundamentally consistent with the Bush administration's new policy of advancing India's economic transformation and growth in national power, objectives that are not only important to India but ultimately crucial to the United States as well. Given the changing capital intensity of Indian development, liberalized access to nuclear, space-related, and dual-use high technology would have palpable consequences for the *pace* of Indian expansion, even if the general direction of growth were likely to continue upward in any event. To the degree that new U.S. policies in the nuclear arena and elsewhere underwrote faster Indian economic growth, they would provide an unparalleled demonstration of American friendship and support. In pursuing such policies, the administration would not only take a major step toward strengthening India's geopolitical importance, but would increase its enthusiasm for contributing toward counterproliferation activities in the Indian Ocean, buttress its potential utility as a hedge against a rising China, encourage it to pursue economic and strategic policies aligned with U.S. interests, and shape its choices in regard to global energy stability and environmental protection.

Using power to prevent some countries from securing controlled technologies, even as Washington helps others acquire them, is eminently defensible—so long as it comports with critical U.S. national interests.

The importance of these goals, however, cannot disguise the fact that permitting India to acquire either nuclear fuel or nuclear technology (the fourth and .fifth options, discussed earlier under the heading "Integrating India into the Global Nuclear Regime") represents a collision with the current universal nonproliferation order. Given U.S. interests that transcend India, the solution to this conundrum cannot consist of jettisoning the regime, but, rather, selectively applying it in practice. This will mean settling, as Richard N. Haass once put it in a private conversation, for a "proliferation of proliferation policies," in which different countries are treated differently based on their friendship toward and value to the United States. Such a strategy obviously requires coordination with U.S. allies and others, a matter the Bush administration ought to focus on as it fieshes out the president's new policy toward India insofar as it bears on global nonproliferation. Seeking exceptions while still trying to maintain universal goals need not weaken the larger nonproliferation order if the United States uses its power artfully to bring along leading countries within the regime, especially in key cartels such as the NSG. Usingpower to prevent some countries from securing controlled technologies, even as Washington helps others acquire them, is eminently defensible—so long as it comports with critical U.S. national interests. If nonproliferation were the sole U.S. strategic objective, or if India did not matter in this regard and others, such inconsistency would be intolerable. Precisely because this is not the case, however, enhanced cooperation in civilian nuclear technology, civilian space programs, and dual-use industrial components becomes a compromise the United States ought to settle for—however reluctantly —given India's importance for the success of U.S. nonproliferation goals and other vital U.S. geopolitical objectives.

The Strategic Dialogue

The strategic dialogue proposed by Secretary of State Rice remains the second critical avenue for securing the growth of U.S.-Indian relations over the long term. It is important to remember that the United States and India have had a strategic dialogue, conducted at both the under secretary and assistant secretary levels, since at least 2001. When instituted, this forum was intended to become the mechanism by which both sides could engage in a serious high-level conversation on global issues with the intent of increasing practical cooperation. During 2001-2003, when the bilateral relationship was at its most intense, the strategic dialogue possessed an intimacy that was displayed in the willingness of both sides to engage in genuinely freewheeling conversation rather than scripted recitation of talking points. Success during this period was enhanced by then–U.S. ambassador to India Robert D. Blackwill's insistence that the U.S. government routinely brief senior officials in New Delhi on major American policy initiatives completely unrelated to bilateral relations, such as discussions with Russia, China, and the European allies on President Bush's New Strategic Framework and sensitive talks within the Organization for the Prohibition of Chemical Weapons. Whenever possible, the United States provided India with advance intimation of major presidential initiatives as well.

This deliberate sharing of information, even on issues that did not involve U.S.-Indian relations directly, provided tangible evidence to Indian policy makers that Washington regarded New Delhi as a true strategic partner, keeping it apprised of developments that involved third parties and, in the process, implicitly underscoring the conviction that India mattered to the United States not just within South Asia but on a global scale. Unfortunately, since 2003, with the expanding crisis in Iraq and the gradual growth of Islamabad's importance relative to New Delhi's in regard to Operation Enduring Freedom, the strategic dialogue between the United States and India has become increasingly anodyne, with the focus of conversation gradually being restricted to the Indian subcontinent rather than the global arena as was the case previously.

The renewed strategic dialogue proposed by Secretary Rice provides an opportunity to reanimate the conversation and restore its quality to reflect the Bush administration's intention of furthering India's growth as a global power. Toward that end, three process-related elements would conduce greatly to the success of the dialogue. *First*, the conversation should be conducted at the highest possible bureaucratic level on both sides to ensure that decision makers, rather than decision executors, have a chance to discuss issues of critical relevance. The choice of Philip Zelikow, counselor to the secretary of state, to lead the U.S. delegation to the strategic dialogue is an inspired one, given Zelikow's familiarity with India (he led the Aspen Strategy Group's colloquy with the Confederation of Indian Industry), his geopolitical vision, and, most important, his bureaucratic clout within the State Department and ready access to Rice. *Second*, the previous practice of confidentially briefing the Indian government on the administration's initiatives both internationally and vis-à-vis third parties—preferably before any public announcement —should be restored. *Third*, the strategic dialogue should include the equivalent of a "high policy forum," where senior policy makers on both sides can engage in unscripted conversations on matters of mutual interest, apart from whatever the formal agenda may require.

The substance of the strategic dialogue ought to focus on the broad issue areas of international and regional order. As far as issues of international order are concerned, .five agenda items deserve priority in the near term: India's membership in the UN Security Council; India's participation in the Proliferation Security Initiative; the character of U.S.-Indian defense cooperation; the nature of the U.S.-Indian partnership in space; and the strengthening of U.S.-Indian cybersecurity cooperation.

Security Council Membership

The question of India's permanent membership on the UN Security Council (UNSC) is a high and pressing priority for New Delhi. All elements along the Indian political spectrum are united in the belief that their country's .flourishing transition from colonialism, its successful incubation of democracy amid incredible cultural and linguistic diversity, its large population, and growing economic prowess justify global recognition through membership in the most important institution of international governance, the UN Security Council. Indians point to fact that their country is a charter member of the United Nations, has a distinguished record of participation in international institutions, and has contributed regularly to UN peacekeeping operations—often in very challenging environments—from the very beginning of the organization's existence.

There are good reasons why the United States ought to affirm its support for New Delhi's membership in the Security Council.

The United States thus far has been reluctant to endorse India's claim to permanent membership in the Security Council. When pressed on this issue during the April 14, 2005, visit of Indian Foreign Minister K. Natwar Singh to Washington, Secretary Rice cautiously responded that "the United States wants to be supportive of what we see as a positive trend in India's global role because India is a democracy and that matters to us in the global role that it is beginning to play. We are demonstrating that we support that aspiration by the breadth of the relationship that we have with India....Now, in terms of the UN Security Council, the United States has said that we believe UN Security Council reform needs to take place in the context of broader UN reform, that it is important, of course, to reform the Secretariat, the institutions of the UN, the organizations of the UN, it needs management reform and, of course, we should also look at Security Council reform. I said when I was in India that international organizations in general will have to take into account India's growing role in the world in order to be updated and to be effective."16 This carefully evasive response was conditioned, in part, by uncertainty about the future shape and direction of UN reform itself. But it was also—and more fundamentally—shaped by two larger administration concerns: whether an expanded Security Council would be conducive to American well-being, and whether having India —with its penchant for pursuing independent foreign policies sometimes at odds with U.S. preferences —as a permanent member of a recon figured Security Council would advance American interests over the long term. Since there is in fact a strong case to be made for *contracting* the Security Council rather than expanding it at this juncture in history, Washington has been deliberately obscure about its own preferences with respect to increasing council membership, preferring to hide behind the position that this is an issue requiring more rejection and discussion within the international community. U.S. concerns about this matter are so significant that until very recently Washington refrained from endorsing even the claims of its own allies: Although it has now publicly affirmed its support for Japan's demand for a council seat, it still reserves judgment on Germany's claim, even though a reasonable case can be made that both countries share a comparable right to Security Council membership.

There are good reasons why the United States ought to, upon rejection, affirm its support for New Delhi's membership in the Security Council. By all contemporary assessments, India is likely to assume a place among the .five major economies in the global system during the .first half of this century. While estimates differ on when India will overtake giants such as Japan, Germany, the United Kingdom, and France by exchange rate measures, all studies agree that India's economy will grow larger than that of each of these countries at some point during the next twenty-five to .fifty years. Analyses by the Central Intelligence Agency indicate that when countries are ranked by composite measures of national power—that is, weighted combinations of gross domestic product (GDP), defense spending, population, and technology growth—India is projected to possess the fourth most capable concentration of power by 2015—after the United States, the European Union, and China—and to be the most important "swing state" in the international system. If global institutions of order are supposed to reflect the material distribution of power—as they must if they are to be relevant—then Washington will be unable to indefinitely avoid entertaining India's claims to Security Council membership without structurally undermining both the evolving hierarchy of international governance and the transformation of U.S.-Indian relations.

If expansion of the Security Council is bound to occur

(because the current structure has outlived the postwar realities that gave birth to it), then the United States will have to live with a different, larger, and potentially more intractable body in any case. Washington can respond to this reality in one of two ways: Either it can gradually move away from the UN system itself as an instrument for advancing U.S. policy goals, or it can refocus on leading the international system by consensus, in effect making the effort required to persuade the new Security Council to support its interests. In either case, India's permanent council membership would pose few disadvantages for the United States.

If Washington settles for a strategy of neglecting the United Nations because that body is too unwieldy and too unhelpful to U.S. objectives, supporting permanent membership for India will entail no costs to the United States. If, in contrast, Washington settles on a strategy of exercising primacy through, among other things, leading the formation of an international consensus when required, India's presence on the Security Council would likely be beneficial to the United States because there are no inherent confects of interest on fundamental questions between the two countries. India would continue to be available as a potential partner in any future "coalition of the willing," and its propensity to play this role would only be enhanced if Washington were seen to promote India's quest for status enhancement in various international bodies. Even when Indian and American interests diverged—as they often do on a variety of matters, including strategies for securing common goals—India's presence on the council would demand no more attention or resources than would be applied to winning over member states truly opposed to U.S. aims. Even the prospect of U.S.-Indian differences in the Security Council, therefore, would likely impose few consequential burdens on the United States. Accordingly, the administration ought to support India's candidacy for permanent membership in the Security Council if expansion is inevitable. Further, and contrary to some of the proposals circulating on this subject, the U.S. government should not dilute the significance of this endorsement with churlish caveats that would deny New Delhi those veto rights associated with full membership. Rather, Washington ought to remain silent on this issue until structural questions about the character of council expansion are settled to U.S. satisfaction at the United Nations.

Core Group Status in the Proliferation Security Initiative

In the context of reforming the international order, the United States should also endorse India's full participation in the administration's newest counterproliferation program, the Proliferation Security Initiative (PSI). The PSI is an effort by a group of like-minded states to aggressively interdict traffic in WMD, including components and delivery systems, on land, in the air, and at sea. The PSI consists of eleven founding participants—Australia, France, Germany, Italy, Japan, the Netherlands, Poland, Portugal, Spain, the United Kingdom, and the United States. Although U.S. officials repeatedly emphasize that the PSI is "an activity, not an organization,"17 that claim is often undermined by the distinction made between a "core group" and other states that vary in their commitment and participation. Despite some reservations about the political and legal basis of the PSI, India has expressed an interest in participating in its activities. New Delhi has in fact undertaken important PSIlike activities on its own, for example, intercepting a major North Korean shipment of missile parts on the high seas. The United States' unwillingness to integrate India into the core group, however, has left New Delhi change about the prospect of joining yet another stratified institution in which it would be accorded only "second-class" status.

The issue of admitting India into the core group was discussed with the United States during Colin Powell's last visit to India as secretary of state. After some debate, Secretary Powell decided not to invite India into the core group because he was influenced by erroneous internal arguments that India remains a serious nonproliferation problem. A careful examination of the evidence on this issue, going back several years, would demonstrate the falsity of this claim. Although India has yet to reach closure on a few proliferation-related cases to U.S. satisfaction, the contention that New Delhi has been a deliberate proliferator is absurd. India certainly ought to be challenged to bring its export control regulations up to international standards and to enforce those laws vigorously—objectives that would be greatly served by more liberal access to various controlled technologies—but its proliferation record is in many respects better than that of some of the PSI's core members. Consequently, there is no reason why India should be excluded from this inner circle. The case for inclusion only grows stronger when New Delhi's naval and air capabilities are considered in the context of potential interdiction operations in the northern Indian Ocean: There is simply no other littoral state in that part of the world whose armed services possess the reach, quality, professionalism, and readiness of the Indian military. Furthermore, at a time when U.S. forces are stretched thin because of the vast demands imposed by stability operations worldwide, the case for incorporating Indian resources into the PSI for both symbolic *and* practical reasons is self-evident. Secretary of State Rice would take an important step in the ongoing transformation of U.S.-Indian relations if she were to correct the decision of her predecessor regarding India—assuming that the United States intends to persist with preserving a core group within the PSI.

Increasing Defense Cooperation

Accelerating the renewal of U.S.-Indian defense cooperation ought to remain the third issue in the strategic dialogue insofar as it pertains to the international order. There is little doubt that defense relations between the two countries have experienced an explosive growth since the waiver of U.S. sanctions imposed after India's May 1998 nuclear tests. The greatest achievements have been in the area of military-to-military ties, exemplified through bilateral exercises, personnel exchanges, high-level and unit visits, military education and training, and officer and unit exchanges. In contrast to these successes—which will only increase as more intense and complex activities are consummated over time—there have been less impressive results in three other areas: sales of major combat systems, bilateral defense industrial collaboration, and combined military operations. The traditional reluctance of the United States to license high-leverage military technologies to India for fear of undermining the regional military balance with Pakistan, in combination with New Delhi's worries about Washington's reliability as a supplier, has prevented defense trade from expanding as much as military-to-military cooperation has. The Bush administration's recent decision to treat India as relevant to a much larger canvas of U.S. interests than South Asia has resulted in the offer of sophisticated aircraft such as the F-16 and the F-18, as well as other transformative capabilities such as command and control, early warning, and missile defense systems. In an effort to ease New Delhi's concerns about reliability, Washington has even expressed willingness to consider licensing coproduction of some of these technologies in India. This is a major—and welcome—step toward improved prospects for increased defense trade. Washington should similarly offer expeditious licensing for sales (or coproduction or "hot transfers" when relevant) of P-3 Orion antisubmarine warfare aircraft, utility and attack helicopters, jet engines, minesweeping vessels, amphibious ships, and excess surface combatants, items currently of great interest to India.

In the realm of missile defense in particular, the Bush administration should offer the Patriot PAC-3 missile—as opposed to merely the Patriot PAC-2—for sale to India, if New Delhi wishes to acquire an American antitactical ballistic missile system. Concurrently, the United States should drop its reluctance to approve an Israeli sale of the Arrow antitactical ballistic missile, because if India chooses to defend a few critical conurbations against missile attacks, it will almost certainly require at least a two-layered terminal defense architecture.

Given the density and diversity of the missile threat New Delhi has to counter, a singlelayered late terminal defense system, even if configured around the advanced PAC-3, will simply be insufficiently for high-confidence protection of the small target set of interest to India. Since the Arrow has been designed for high endoatmospheric defense—and could be integrated with the Patriot for low endoatmospheric protection—a two-layered architecture would provide the perfect technical combination for Indian defense planners. Finally, the economic benefits to Israel of U.S. assent to an Arrow sale to India ought not to be lost on senior administration officials.

Even before sales of such systems are contemplated, however, the United States should provide much more technical assistance to India than is currently under way with respect to missile defense requirements analysis, since defense technologists and planners in New Delhi need to acquire a realistic sense of what missile defenses can and cannot do in the specific threat environment facing India today and over the long term. Consequently, satisfying the current Indian interest in technical information pertinent to requirements and evaluation, followed by joint development in certain limited areas, would be very useful to both sides, even before security managers in New Delhi made any decisions pertaining to the acquisition of complete missile defense systems.

So long as Washington abides by its new intention to facilitate the growth of Indian power, and, accordingly, does not limit the sale of U.S. weaponry to India to comport with some illusory criterion of maintaining a military "balance" with

Pakistan—an untenable proposition, given the disparity in national capabilities between the two sides, and a dangerous one as well, insofar as it disregards the Chinese security threat to India —there is every reason to expect that U.S.-Indian defense trade will grow in much the same way military-to-military cooperation has thus far. What the United States ought to encourage, as a response to Indian concerns about the reliability of supply and transfer of technology and the American desire to improve the trade balance between the two sides, is increased investment by American companies in India's defense industry. The Indian defense-industrial complex, which until recently was closed entirely to foreign companies and barely open even to Indian private enterprise, has now been partially liberalized, with New Delhi soliciting foreign direct investment (FDI) up to a limit of twenty-six percent of equity. The United States should press India through the strategic and economic dialogues to extend these limits to at least .fifty-one percent, if not abolish them entirely, while encouraging American private investment through the promise of liberalized licensing under the U.S. Department of State's International Traffic in Arms Regulations and Munitions List rules.

There are many areas where such liberalization can occur without compromising U.S. national security. What India needs most often are not the "big-ticket" weapons that galvanize public attention but high-quality subassemblies and components that make a difference to the durability and effectiveness of existing inventory or major systems currently under development. U.S.-Indian defense industrial collaboration for the foreseeable future could therefore be dominated by a variety of niche activities. These ought not involve threats to American technological leadership but should nonetheless produce the desirable consequence of integrating U.S. industry into India's defense modernization efforts. In this context, the strategic dialogue should in tandem with the existing Defense Policy Group (DPG), direct the Joint Technical Group, which operates under the aegis of the DPG, to increase collaborative defense research, development, and production, especially in those areas where India has a comparative advantage.

While the purpose of defense cooperation is to advance the growth of Indian power, such collaboration must pay equal attention to how the United States and India can join forces to undertake combined military operations in the future—either under the aegis of the United Nations or outside it. In many ways, much of the U.S.-Indian defense cooperation thus far has been oriented to increasing mutual familiarity between the two armed forces in order to advance the goal of interoperability. But with furthering the growth of Indian power now a conscious U.S. objective, more heed should be paid to how New Delhi's military resources could be used collaboratively to advance the national interests of both countries. The Indian efforts during the Straits of Malacca patrols in support of Operation Enduring Freedom and the closely coordinated activities in relief operations in the aftermath of the December 2004 tsunami in southern and southeastern Asia provide examples of how both countries could cooperate in ad hoc coalitions of the willing outside any formal UN mandate. The Indian Navy's escort operations at Malacca in the aftermath of the 9/11 attacks were precedent setting in this regard. And if the Vajpayee government had made the decision to contribute an Indian Army division to Iraqi stabilization operations—a decision it came very close to but ultimately could not make because of the controversies surrounding Operation Iraqi Freedom in Indian domestic politics—the notion of combined operations between the two countries would have received an incredible fillip, as would the transformation in bilateral relations.

In any event, the time is ripe for both sides to think innovatively about combined operations, and these do not need to be precipitated solely by natural disasters or geopolitical crises. Given the current strain on U.S. military forces, for example, there is no reason why the United States and India cannot formalize a memorandum of understanding on cooperative military operations in the Indian Ocean. Through that body of water passes a variety of high-value traffic, some of which requires constant surveillance. Given India's geographic advantages and its military capabilities, a cooperative division of labor with respect to ocean surveillance, search and rescue, anti-piracy operations, and humanitarian assistance would be a good place to start. These activities could be undertaken even without a memorandum of understanding, but they would then be at risk of being entirely ad hoc and lacking integration with larger U.S. purposes. A formal agreement, therefore, has the advantage of engendering stable cooperation, defining formally understood obligations, and leading to increases in mutual confidence that could pave the way for more ambitious combined operations.

It is appropriate for the United States and India now to think about signing a comprehensive defense partnership agreement.

Given the achievements in military-to-military relations during the last four years, it is also appropriate for the United States and India now tothink about signing a comprehensive defense partnership agreement, of which the memorandum of understanding that governs combined military operations would be a part. The last time both countries formally initialed any major defense accord was in 1995 when the Agreed Minute on Defense Relations between the United States and India was signed in New Delhi on January 12 of that year. The Agreed Minute was an important waypoint in the evolution of bilateral defense cooperation: it created institutions to manage the defense relationship that survive to this day. Given the dramatic advances of the last few years, however, the Agreed Minute now appears overly limited and hence ought to be replaced by a new framework that is explicitly focused on improving Indian military capabilities to service larger bilateral strategic objectives. This new defense partnership agreement ought to integrate U.S. and Indian interests in the areas of military-to-military relations, defense trade and production, joint research and development, and combined operations, into a single document that defines both an ambitious vision for the new strategic relationship and a roadmap for realizing its goals over time.

Enhanced Cooperation on Space

The fourth major issue, insofar as it pertains to discussion within the strategic dialogue on international matters, is U.S.-Indian cooperation in regard to space. India's space program is the crown jewel of its technological achievements in the post-Independence period. Begun in 1962 with the specific intention of pursuing only scientific and developmental endeavors, the founding father of the program, Vikram Sarabhai, was a committed pacifist in the Gandhian mold who went to great lengths to insulate his organization from the Indian nuclear program, then headed by Homi Bhabha. From the beginning, the Indian space program sought and maintained strong links with the U.S. National Aeronautics and Space Administration. This relationship helped the Indian Space Research Organization (ISRO) become a worldclass program characterized by a strong culture of professionalism, internal accountability, and high technical standards. Not surprisingly, within three decades ISRO developed an impressive end-toend space capability that included production of a variety of launch vehicles and remote sensing, communication, and meteorological satellites; acquisition of systems engineering expertise; and maintenance of the organizational and technical infrastructure necessary to control space assets.

As American nonproliferation concerns began to grow during the 1970s and 1980s, U.S.-Indian space cooperation progressively diminished. It was entirely extinguished in regard to space launch vehicles (SLVs), which were perceived by successive U.S. administrations as more or less identical to ballistic missiles. Consequently, India continued its indigenous efforts to develop SLVs, aided whenever possible by small clandestine acquisitions of foreign technologies. Before long, ISRO became capable of launching larger and larger payloads into space and in the process was transformed into a serious competitor in commercial launch services involving low earth orbits. While civilian activities related to communications, broadcasting, remote sensing, meteorology, distance education, telemedicine, natural resources management, space science, and satellite launch services dominate ISRO's programmatic agenda, the organization was compelled by Indian policy makers during the early 1980s to help the Defense Research and Development Organization develop the solid-fuel rockets needed by India's missile program. This assistance, which materialized in the form of interorganizational personnel exchanges, sharing of facilities, and ISRO production of the Daisy solidpropellant motors for India's Agni series missiles, undermined the organization's traditional claim of involvement solely in the peaceful uses of space, and thereby justified a series of U.S. decisions to constrain cooperation with ISRO even on what were admittedly nonmilitary endeavors.

NSSP represented the first serious U.S. effort in decades to review these constraints with an eye to increasing U.S.-Indian space cooperation. Aided by the fact that U.S. legislative restraints and international regime commitments were less onerous in this area (compared, for example, to nuclear technology), NSSP made major policy advances by defining a road map that would permit India to acquire a variety of dual-use technologies needed by its space program; to jointly develop, produce, operate, and market commercial satellites; and eventually to launch either foreign satellites containing U.S. components or U.S. satellites themselves upon successful conclusion of a space cooperation agreement. This enhanced collaboration was premised on the belief that U.S.- Indian space partnership was possible in a wide range of areas, except for SLV technology and high-resolution remote sensing, so long as New Delhi met two conditions: agreeing to undertake a comprehensive upgrade of its export control system and promising not to use the artifacts acquired through NSSP liberalization to advance its own strategic weapon programs.

While the first condition is eminently sensible as a precondition for enhanced U.S.-Indian space cooperation, the second potentially runs counter to the Bush administration's new interest in assisting the growth of Indian power. If helping India become a major player on the Asian stage is to have any meaning, it implies lending New Delhi a hand with respect to developing its national power comprehensively. The administration, accordingly, has decided to support India with its conventional military capabilities, economic growth, and energy production. But existing U.S. policies threaten to crimp India's ability to develop certain strategic assets, an outcome that would at the end of the day undermine the larger American objective of advancing the growth of Indian power in Asia. The Bush administration must review these policies during its second term if its fundamental intention to help India increase its national power is not to be inadvertently (or deliberately) frustrated.

Two specific and long-standing policies cry out for

immediate review and reform: The first pertains to current U.S. prejudices against India's strategic weapon programs, and the second to the issue of internal versus external proliferation insofar as it affects U.S. technology transfers to India.

If the United States is serious about advancing its geopolitical objectives in Asia, it would almost by definition help New Delhi develop its strategic capabilities such that India's nuclear weaponry and associated delivery systems could deter against the growing and utterly more capable nuclear forces Beijing is likely to possess by 2025. In a previous generation, the United States assisted the British and French nuclear weapon programs in critical ways so as to deny the Soviet Union permanent strategic immunity vis-à-vis these two smaller states. U.S. aid to the French nuclear weapon program is particularly pertinent: first, because it occurred despite President Charles de Gaulle's withdrawal of France from the unified military command of the North Atlantic Treaty Organization (NATO); and second, because of the form it took, namely, the quiet but effective practice of "negative guidance,"[18] through which U.S. weapon scientists were able to tell their French counterparts when and how they were in error, even if the Americans could not always provide the French with the information to remedy those mistakes. While there is clearly a world of difference between the U.S.-French and the U.S.-Indian relationships, there is good reason to believe that the latter may come to resemble the former at some point because of the anticipated growth of Chinese power. If this turns out to be the case, the only strong argument against U.S.- Indian cooperation in strategic weaponry will be not that it is undesirable, but that it is premature. And, of course, there is no denying that there are myriad treaty, legislative, and bureaucratic constraints on such cooperation—currently. It also does not require much imagination to appreciate that if the impediments to bilateral civilian nuclear cooperation are already so burdensome, the obstacles to collaborative strategic weapon development must be even more so.

This likely condition notwithstanding, there is one important way in which the United States can extend its acquiescence to the development of India's strategic programs, even if it cannot support those actively in the near term—by refraining from all *diplomatic* actions that undermine New Delhi's effort to improve its strategic weaponry. For example, there is no reason whatsoever why the Bush administration, as a matter of presidential policy, could not decide that during its second term it would simply:

- eschew issuing gratuitous public statements urging India to sign the NPT as a non-nuclear weapon state
- abstain from condemning India's missile research, development, test, and evaluation activities
- cease to demarche foreign governments to restrain their national entities involved in supporting India's nuclear, missile, and space programs
- refrain from denouncing India's strategic acquisition and deployment decisions so long as these did not violate sensible principles relating to the security and survivability of its nuclear deterrent

If the administration were to settle for even such conservative reforms as these, it would not only send an important signal to India about larger American intentions but would *materially* contribute to preserving the future balance of power in Asia—a prospect that motivated former U.S. ambassador to India Robert D. Blackwill to ask recently, "Why should the U.S. want to check India's missile capability in ways that could lead to China's permanent nuclear dominance over democratic India?"19 Even if the United States cannot actively aid India in developing its strategic capabilities, it ought to pursue policies having exactly that effect. Currently, the easiest way for the administration to do this is simply to leave New Delhi—and its international partners—alone.

U.S. policy on the second issue, internal versus external proliferation, also needs urgent reform. As noted earlier in the present work (under the heading "NSSP as a Hesitant Revolution," and subsequently) the advances enshrined in NSSP on liberalizing India's access to dual-use, space, and civilian nuclear technologies were premised on the understanding that New Delhi would create an export control system that prevented all kinds of leakage, either deliberate or inadvertent, to foreign entities, while it simultaneously refrained from using U.S.- origin technologies to advance its own strategic programs. The former requirement, pertaining to external proliferation, should be enforced energetically because it is in neither U.S. nor Indian interests for sensitive technologies to seep out to third parties or otherwise get leaked in any unlawful way. The latter condition, pertaining to internal proliferation, while necessary at the time for successfully concluding NSSP, ought to be abolished by the Bush administration, for four reasons.

First, the ban on using U.S.-origin technologies to advance Indian strategic programs is in fact *astrategic*, in that it is inconsistent with the objective of advancing the growth of Indian power in those critical technological arenas important to the preservation of the geopolitical balance in Asia.

Second, it imposes unreasonable burdens on India, in that it requires New Delhi to sustain arti official rewalls *within* its national technological system, with the enclave focused on strategic programs unable either to draw from or contribute to the activities of the nonstrategic sector merely because the latter happens to enjoy access to foreign technologies—even though both segments are supported by the same set of taxpayers and advance the national objectives of the same sovereign, namely, the people of India. Such .rewalls, even if they could be erected, would be difficult to sustain indefinitely and would become the object of constant circumvention even assuming the Indian government's best intentions.

Third, it creates gratuitous irritants in the bilateral relationship with India: By preventing Indian national organizations that are formally assigned by their government to develop certain strategic capabilities from meeting those programmatic goals (which do not in any event threaten U.S. security), the emphasis on preventing internal proliferation puts the United States and India at odds, with no discernible benefit to American interests. Even worse, it requires less-than-transparent U.S. intelligence assets to perform policing functions to determine whether and how various Indian organizations might be violating the prohibitions against internal proliferation, while at the same time denying the Indian government—thanks to legitimate concerns about protecting sources and methods—the full information required to corroborate U.S. claims in a way that would stand scrutiny when challenged by various democratic institutions such as India's press, courts, and Parliament.

Secretary Rice should move decisively to change current U.S. diplomatic practices that exemplify a prejudice against India's SLV development efforts in particular and its strategic programs in general.

Fourth, it ensures defeat on the installment plan. If Indian national interests demand the acquisition of certain strategic capabilities such as nuclear weapons and their associated delivery systems, and American national interests do not permit a complete technological quarantine of India, then the current U.S. obsession with preventing internal proliferation will only become increasingly unsustainable over time. Because their national goals demand the acquisition of certain material assets, entities in the Indian strategic enclaves will develop formal and informal means of obtaining U.S. technologies imported into the country, and any American attempt to prevent such access will only engender even more ingenious strategies to defeat it. Thanks in part to the character of technology itself, U.S. efforts to thwart internal proliferation between entities of the same government will spawn cat-and-mouse games that repeatedly come to grief and waste American energies and resources with no worthwhile gains for U.S. national interests.

Where space cooperation is concerned, therefore, Secretary Rice should move decisively to change current U.S. diplomatic practices that exemplify a prejudice against India's SLV development efforts in particular and its strategic programs in general, while dropping the bureaucratic concern about internal proliferation, which impedes U.S. technology transfers to India, in favor of a focus on external proliferation alone. If these two initiatives can be implemented, many traditional headaches such as those relating to the presence of Indian organizations on the U.S. Entity List and the Visa Mantis restrictions on Indian nuclear and space scientists travelling to the United States would automatically disappear. Further, it would become relatively easy for Washington to demand that New Delhi adhere to all NSG and Missile Technology Control Regime regulations if these were to become part of the larger quid pro quo governing the new U.S. approach to India's strategic weapon programs.

Expanding Cybersecurity Cooperation

Finally, the strategic dialogue should be used to direct energy and resources toward building on extant achievements in cybersecurity. In November 2001, President Bush and Prime Minister Vajpayee jointly announced the U.S.-Indian Cyber-Terrorism Initiative, a product of the efforts of then-U.S. ambassador Blackwill. The first plenary meeting of the cybersecurity forum occurred soon thereafter, in April 2002.

While it represented an impressive beginning, the enthusiasm for deep engagement with India on cybersecurity matters was less than overwhelming on the U.S. side because of the perception that New Delhi's interests centered primarily on expanding its capacity for information warfare or interdiction of terrorism involving Pakistan. U.S. fears about the .first issue were exaggerated: Although India maintains an offensive information warfare capability, it is relatively small in programmatic terms and of uncertain quality, and has never been able to attract either the resources or the manpower that has .owed into the country's private-sector–dominated information technologies industry. India's concern with interdicting terrorist information operations, by contrast, is undoubtedly strong: Given the scale, diversity, and, increasingly, the sophistication of terrorist networks in India, New Delhi's interest in computer forensics, network surveillance, and the protection of supervisory control and data acquisition systems as means to defeat terrorism is not only understandable but ought to be supported as part of the U.S. global struggle against this menace.

For a variety of reasons, bilateral cooperation in cybersecurity has grown too slowly, in part because of bureaucratic fears in the U.S. government about increasing Indian capacities prematurely. The Bush administration's new policy of assisting in the growth of Indian power ought to provide strategic guidance for sharply increased support of improvements to New Delhi's technical proficiency in countering terrorist information operations, especially since many of the Islamist groups that threaten India treat the United

States as an enemy as well. Accordingly, the new strategic dialogue proposed by Secretary Rice ought to have as a priority expanded U.S.-Indian cybersecurity cooperation in a variety of areas, including critical infrastructure protection, safeguards for national communications systems, assistance with law enforcement, defense information assurance, the development of security standards, and collaboration between government and the private sector.

Along with these strategic reasons for enhanced cybersecurity partnership, there is a vital commercial justification for bringing this initiative to full maturity—the growing importance of information technology in U.S.-Indian trade, and in the increasingly extensive electronic connectivity between the two societies. Of all the areas where the U.S. and Indian economies interlock, information technology and its numerous derivatives remain the most important for both sides. From highend software and technology services to low-end back-office and call center operations, information businesses have enjoyed explosive growth since the late 1990s and have come to define the contours of the bilateral economic relationship. Numerous American .firms now routinely look to India for large supplies of well-educated, English-speaking workers to support their backroom operations, at much lower wages than would be imaginable in the United States. These backroom operations support not only business activities of American corporations in the United States but, increasingly, enterprises in third countries as well. As such, the large and growing American reliance on business process outsourcing to India represents a major new dimension of global economic integration, with India and the United States now symbiotically linked in many commercial activities impossible to conceive as recently as a decade ago. The tremendous cost savings accruing to American businesses as a result of business process outsourcing to India almost certainly ensure the continued vitality of the U.S.-Indian information technologies market, a sector that today generates almost three percent of India's GDP and which is expected to swell .vefold by 2008, becoming a US$57 billion-a-year export industry employing four million people and accounting for seven percent of GDP.

The justification for greater investment in cybersecurity is to be found entirely in these facts. As the American and Indian economies becoming increasingly intertwined, with private U.S. medical, financial, product, research and development, and other data moving rapidly through newer and newer forms of outsourcing, the necessity for state-of-the-art data security becomes imperative. Not only is this essential to the continued growth of the Indian information technology sector, and by implication to the growth of Indian power, it is equally vital to the success of American industry, which increasingly relies on Indian labor for the health of its bottom line, and to the well-being of the American people, who quite reasonably expect that any personal information cycled through India will be protected against unlawful intrusion or compromise. The Indian record thus far has been remarkably good as far as defense against insider threats is concerned: Security at the premier information technology companies is rigorous, with all computers technically configured to prevent data downloading, and camera and mobile phone use inside company facilities pervasively restricted. However, the threat remains of network attacks by external foes—those who possess adversarial national or ideological allegiances and those who do not. The persistence of this threat, as indicated by the continuing high level of computer network–related emergency response activities by the federal government and private corporations in the United States, only underscores the need for robust defenses against information attack and intrusion in India, particularly from external threats that may seek access to privileged data in order to attack larger American interests. The success of globalization as manifested in the explosive growth of the U.S.-Indian information technology trade has thus made cybersecurity *in India* a critical international issue that simultaneously takes on major economic, political, strategic, and even personal dimensions.

In this context, the United States ought to increase the financial resources and high-level attention paid to cybersecurity initiatives currently being discussed with India. During the 2004 plenary meeting of the U.S.-Indian Cybersecurity Forum, the leader of the Indian delegation, Arvind Gupta, emphasized that New Delhi's long-term priorities would consist of capacity building, increased training, and personnel exchange. In short, the focus would be on developing the expertise and technology required for India to master the threats posed to cybersecurity across a range of domains. Toward that end, Gupta proposed that the United States and India jointly create a cybersecurity fund, which would draw on small but equal contributions by the two governments, perhaps supplemented later by the private sector, and which would be used to finance training projects agreed to by the Cybersecurity Forum. He also urged the creation of a multidisciplinary U.S.- Indian cybersecurity training institute, where different dimensions of cyberprotection, including cybersecurity standards and best practices, national laws and enforcement capabilities, data protection issues, prosecution of cybercrime, computer emergency response teams, and national assurance programs for defense and civilian infrastructures, could be examined and developed.

With cybersecurity in the bilateral relationship clearly no longer the exotic issue it seemed when President Bush and Prime Minister Vajpayee first called attention to it in 2001, Gupta's two proposals ought to be speedily implemented after appropriate review in the U.S.-Indian strategic dialogue. As former U.S. under secretary of commerce Kenneth I. Juster told the India-U.S. Information Security Summit in 2004,

> Information security—also known as cybersecurity— is one of the keys to unlocking the full potential of the trade and technology relationship between the United States and India. All levels of society today—from individuals, to companies, to governments—rely on information technology and information networks in their daily lives—to communicate, to manage activities, to transact business, and to provide essential services to the public. As commerce between the United States and India continues to expand, consumers and corporations will seek to ensure that their personal information and business proprietary data are secure, and that information services are reliable and protected. Without an adequate level of security,

we run the risk of backlash among consumers and loss of confidences among business people, which could severely limit progress in our trade and technology relationship.[20]

Managing Regional Security

While the issues of international order in the strategic dialogue span a variety of complex concerns, the problems of regional order—also difficult, but in different ways—are unified by an overarching theme: the need to cope with state failure in almost *every* political entity on India's periphery—Afghanistan, Pakistan, Nepal, Bangladesh, Sri Lanka, and Myanmar.

The problems of regional order are unified by an overarching theme: the need to cope with state failure in almost every political entity on India's periphery.

In Afghanistan, the state-building process, while moving forward, is by no means complete: Central government authority does not yet extend meaningfully throughout the country, a debilitating upsurge in narcotics production threatens the state's future, and the internationally supported economic reconstruction program remains far from fruition. While Afghanistan has witnessed a successful presidential election, the parliamentary process mandated by the Bonn conference has not yet occurred. The state has also not fully mastered the challenges of providing law and order, integrating the warlords into the political process, raising a new national army, and eliminating the Taliban as a threat to the Afghan polity. Yet despite all these difficulties, Afghanistan offers reasons for optimism—though not yet assurances of success—because of the continued U.S. and NATO military presence in the country, the desire of both the country's leaders and its neighbors for peace, and the massive international assistance promised for Afghan renewal. India remains one of the largest international donors to Afghanistan's reconstruction. The challenge for the strategic dialogue would be to find ways to expand those contributions in ways acceptable to both Kabul and New Delhi.

Pakistan too is in the midst of complex changes, and success is by no means a foregone conclusion. The president, General Musharraf, is personally wedded to a doctrine of "enlightened moderation," but he has made numerous compromises with radical Islamist forces and elevated their prominence in national politics during the last several years. Military rule remains entrenched despite lip service to democracy, and the presence of the military and intelligence services has expanded to all areas of national life. The infrastructure supporting the *jihadi* groups warring against India remains intact, and continues to enjoy comprehensive state support despite Pakistan's prominence in the global war against terrorism. Social indicators remain at extremely problematic levels and may even be worsening, even though macroeconomic stability has been restored, albeit in part through large injections of foreign aid. All these facts raise once again the old and uncomfortable question: Will the temporary stability associated with authoritarian rule crumble, with worse consequences for Pakistan in the future? As far as the strategic dialogue is concerned, U.S.-Indian parleys relating to Pakistan ought to be dominated by one issue: How can both sides collaborate with Islamabad in supporting Pakistan's transformation into a stable, moderate state?

The Kingdom of Nepal remains wracked by a bitter civil war. The problems caused by the Maoist insurgency have been exacerbated by King Gyanendra's efforts to claim absolute power despite the apparent fecklessness of both the monarchy and its principal bastion of support, the Royal Nepali Army. The Maoists, who represent the most important threat to the monarchy, already control more than two-thirds of the kingdom, with state institutions virtually absent in most rural areas. Finally, it is not at all evident that the king's most recent effort at rule by decree will eliminate the corruption and mismanagement that characterized Nepali governance during rule by an absolute monarch, from 1960 to 1991. Nepal, which occupies a strategic location along the Himalayan foothills dividing China and India, thus appears to be cascading toward state failure, with serious consequences not only for current U.S. policy but for stable Sino-Indian relations as well. Given this context, the U.S.-Indian strategic dialogue ought to focus on ways of deepening the excellent existing bilateral collaboration on Nepal so as to shepherd the kingdom toward a return to democracy and help it devise better ways to defeat the Maoist insurgency that threatens all three countries in different ways.

Bangladesh remains a dangerous example of a growing

failure of governance caused by political paralysis. The vicious, uncompromising struggle for power between the two principal political parties, now manifesting itself in targeted assassinations and street violence, has produced a political miasma in which the decline of law and order, rampant corruption, bureaucratic incompetence, and growing human insecurity are increasingly exacerbated by the rise of Islamic fundamentalist groups. Despite much international assistance, the dangerous trends associated with confrontational politics in Bangladesh have accelerated at a frightening rate, threatening to rend the social fabric, retard democracy and economic advancement, and provide a fertile environment for the rise of "muscle men," and possibly of terrorist groups with larger regional ambitions. Neither the government nor the opposition currently appears to have either the competence or the motivation to set these problems right. The strategic dialogue will have achieved a major success if it enables the United States to acquire a better appreciation of the dangerous descent into crisis that defines Bangladesh's trajectory as a state. The dialogue could also serve as a forum where both the United States and India could coordinate their strategies for dealing with what could be the next major case of political implosion in South Asia.

The civil war in Sri Lanka has spawned one of the world's most vicious separatist movements, the Liberation Tigers of Tamil Eelam, and has claimed the lives of tens of thousands since 1983. The peace process between the two sides, mediated by Norway, has ground to a halt, as neither party appears willing to make the concessions required for a viable federal solution that would provide the Tamils with autonomy while preserving the state's integrity. Although a cease-fire initiated in 2003 is still holding—precariously—there appears to be no prospect of a permanent solution. Even if a way out is found eventually, there is no denying that Sri Lanka, known as "Serendip" to longago Arab geographers, and until recently one of South Asia's more advanced and prosperous states, has been permanently scarred by the two decades of violence. The challenge to participants in the strategic dialogue in these circumstances is simply to .find collaborative ways of encouraging both the Sri Lankan government and the Liberation Tigers of Tamil Eelam to hold to the cease-fire even as national political trends hopefully will evolve in the direction of making federal solutions to the crisis more viable over time.

Myanmar (Burma) continues in the iron grip of the abominable military junta now known as the SPDC, as it has been for more than a decade. The excesses of the regime, manifested in systematic abuses of human rights and the refusal to transfer power to the legally elected government of the country—the party led by Nobel Peace Prize recipient Aung San Suu Kyi—have continued despite great international opposition and even a UN charge of "crimes against humanity." The isolation of the regime has resulted in a growing relationship with China, which has used the opportunity to increase its influence through military and economic assistance, stepped-up Sinicization along Myanmar's northern frontier, growing infrastructure investments, and a nascent military presence along the Andaman Sea coast. These developments do not augur well either for Myanmar's evolution as a democratic state or for the balance of power in the region. Myanmar represents a tough challenge for the U.S.-Indian strategic dialogue because the approaches being taken by the United States and India are at some variance. The regional security component of the discussions should be used as an opportunity for Washington and New Delhi to modify their current strategies so as to reach political goals that are common to both sides—restoring democracy and limiting the growth of Chinese influence in Myanmar.

India remains an island of democratic values and political stability in a region convulsed by religious fanaticism, illiberal governments, state sponsors of terrorism, and economic stasis.

If only because of sheer proximity, India is the entity most affected by the string of state failures in southern and southeastern Asia. But as the example of 9/11 demonstrates, the United States may not be very far behind if the arteries of globalization allow one or more of the region's many disaffected groups to export violence beyond their immediate confines. For these reasons, the United States and India ought to pay special attention to developing common, or at least consistent, strategies for dealing with problems related to state failure in the region. Thus far, the U.S.-Indian partnership has been most effective in regard to Nepal, Afghanistan, and Sri Lanka, in that order; it has been virtually nonexistent concerning Bangladesh, where Washington has been slow to recognize the dimensions of the emerging problem. The two partners' interests have been divergent, almost competitive, in regard to Myanmar and Pakistan.

The renewed strategic dialogue offers an opportunity to shore up these areas of weakness and to set the process of cooperation on firmer foundations by basing U.S. regional policy on the recognition that India's safety and success are strategic assets to the United States. India remains an island of democratic values and political stability in a region convulsed by religious fanaticism, illiberal governments, state sponsors of terrorism, and economic stasis. The fact that India's democratic political system has managed to peacefully integrate the aspirations of close to 150 million Muslims at a time of worldwide Islamist ferment remains a tribute to the accomplishment of the Indian political experiment. The sheer scale of democracy in India—where more than a billion people speaking fifteen different languages and more than 600 dialects peaceably associate through a complex federal system and regularly return to the polls to elect new governments—ought to underscore the point that an India that joined its neighbors in succumbing to state failure or was threatened by its neighbors' pathologies would be catastrophic for U.S. interests, if only because it would release disaffected individuals onto the world stage on a scale that would make many other contemporary challenges look small in comparison. The strategic dialogue, therefore, ought to become a venue where both sides can discuss and harmonize their policies to produce regional outcomes that advance common objectives.

The Economic Dialogue

Renewing the economic dialogue is the third area of activity in the Bush administration's recent initiative vis-à-vis India. The conversation on economic issues itself is not new: The original U.S.-Indian economic dialogue was inaugurated by President Clinton and Prime Minister Vajpayee in March 2000. During their meeting of November 9, 2001, President Bush and Prime Minister Vajpayee announced the expansion and intensification of this discussion, adding separate energy and environmental components to the three original pillars, which were focused on finance, commerce, and trade. Bush and Vajpayee also signaled their intention to significantly enhance privatesector interaction in order to broaden and deepen ties between the Indian and American business communities and to enable the government-to government discussions to benefit more fully from these communities' practical and specific experiences. During the Vajpayee government's tenure (1998–2004), the director of the U.S. National Economic Council, Larry Lindsey, and India's national security adviser, Brajesh Mishra, coordinated and led the dialogue, with Under Secretary of State Alan Larson and Prodipto Ghosh, additional secretary in the Prime Minister's Office, serving as executive secretaries.

While several meetings of the economic dialogue have taken place between various principals in different venues, the process itself has produced lackluster results thus far. This outcome is unfortunate because economic growth provides the critical foundation for national power, and India cannot expect to take its place among the major states in the international system without a sustained improvement in economic performance that lasts many decades. More to the point, it is now clear to India's political leaders that sustained economic growth itself cannot occur without massive expansion of India's connectivity with the international economy. Although the nation's saving rate of twenty-four percent of GDP is impressive in absolute terms, it still falls short of the Asia-Pacific and Chinese benchmarks of thirty-seven and thirty-eight percent, respectively. Even more to the point, a twenty-four percent saving rate is incompatible with India's desired growth of eight percent annually, which is the minimum required if New Delhi is to bridge the employment gap manifested by the millions of people who seek to join the workforce every year but cannot .find the requisite opportunities. These problems can be mitigated only by even steeper increases in growth. But given India's current domestic saving level, elevated growth rates require resources, technology, and managerial skills that only a freer .ow of goods, capital, and labor across borders can provide.

In effect, then, India has to engineer two revolutions in economic management concurrently, if it is to expand its national capabilities sufficiently to propel it into the ranks of the major powers in the international system: (1) a transformation of its domestic economy, primarily through the progressive enthronement of market mechanisms in all sectors so that the relative scarcities of the factors of production are reflected in the prices they command through impersonal bidding in competitive institutions; (2) an expansion of foreign trade and investment through a reduction in tariff and nontariff barriers so that resources from the international system can

.ow into the country to further fuel growth, even as domestic resources are reallocated into the most productive avenues in consonance with the laws of comparative advantage. If these two revolutions are brought to completion within the present decade, India's indigenous pools of capital, labor, and technology will not only be more efficiently used but also supplemented by foreign inputs to sustain and even expand the relatively high levels of growth the country has experienced since at least the early 1990s.

But herein lies the catch: The processes of rapid economic growth are fueled best not by governments seeking to control the process through centralized direction but by impersonal forces of the market, where billions of microdecisions are made by atomistic entities whose only immediate interest is their own utility or profit maximization within some preexisting structure of constraints. In such circumstances, the principal role government can play is to ensure that the overarching constraining structures—the regulations governing the conduct of activities in the marketplace—are fair, transparent, open, and stable. This recipe for economic growth does not in any way minimize the importance of government; rather, it acknowledges that government policy is critical to providing the framework within which productive economic exchanges by private agents can take place. In so doing, it defines what the focus of the renewed economic dialogue between the United States and India ought to be if its future is to avoid resembling its past: namely, altering the structural framework that governs the .ow of economic resources between the two sides through the instruments of policy change. This objective is explicitly based on the recognition that increased economic intercourse between the two sides, if it is to occur, will come about primarily through the decisions of private agents acting outside the direction of governments in search of better profit-seeking opportunities.

The U.S.-Indian economic dialogue, which already has .five pillars and is likely to be augmented with two additional pillars, relating to knowledgebased industries and infrastructure, historically has failed to deliver on its promise for several reasons: The objectives in each pillar were too amorphous and lacked actionable goals; the inherent inequity in economic strength between the two countries resulted even in commonly accepted goals being frustrated because of the differential in costs and benefits accruing to the two sides; the leadership in both countries faced difficulties in regard to institutionalizing policy changes that would alienate core political constituencies; and each side perceived that the other tended to promote only those policies that advantaged it asymmetrically. These problems emphatically do not derive from a lack of goodwill on either side, but arise, rather, from the reality that even sensible policy changes impose near-term costs that may be prohibitive politically. Such constraints will not disappear even in the renewed dialogue but must be confronted and resolved, perhaps piecemeal, because the alternative to expanded market liberalization in India, both domestic and international, is reduced growth, more acute struggles over equity, and eventually a decline in the capacity to accumulate national power.

Three Objectives of the Economic Dialogue

The renewed economic dialogue, which likely will be chaired by India's deputy chairman of the Planning Commission, Montek Singh Ahluwalia, and the chairman of the U.S. National Economic Council, Allan Hubbard, ought to focus on three broad objectives: solving problems, sharing information, and enhancing opportunity.

In regard to the .first objective, the renewed economic dialogue ought to focus on bringing high-level political attention to bear on solving policy problems that cannot be resolved at the working level. Many issues pertaining to regulatory or policy change with respect to internal reform and bilateral trade involve difficult decisions that cannot be made by bureaucracies, no matter how well motivated. The advantage of a high-level dialogue is that it allows the political leadership to intervene, making the choices required from among a range of preexamined options.

For the second objective, the specific focus ought to be on disseminating information about various subject-matter issues relevant to each pillar in the dialogue. While this task may initially seem trivial, it is not. In any complex system, information is costly to obtain, and in complicated issue areas relating to energy, .finance, commerce, infrastructure, and the environment, knowledge about the relevant private and public actors, their interests, and the regulations that affect their activities may be hard to secure. The economic dialogue should help reduce these costs to the advantage of both sides.

The economic dialogue must aim to increase the integration of the American and Indian economies with the intent of maximizing joint gains for both so as to support the rise of Indian power.

Concerning the third objective, the focus should not be solely on discerning new opportunities in traditional economic sectors, but on nontraditional areas as well, such as retailing, education, health care, and entertainment. In traditional areas of the Indian economy such as infrastructure, energy, and agriculture, where increased investment is critical to achieving India's growth objectives and where the desired outlays are large, have lengthy gestation periods, and are often high risk, the economic dialogue can play a critical role by helping to guide the Indian state toward strategic interventions such as providing appropriate guarantees to potential investors, offering specific incentives to particular vendors, and even choosing winners when required—hopefully, rarely—on the basis of the intersecting exigencies of economics and geopolitics.

The substantive goals underlying all these improvements in process must not be lost sight of. The economic dialogue must aim to increase the integration of the American and Indian economies with the intent of maximizing joint gains for both so as to support the rise of Indian power. The bad news historically is that trade between the United States and India has been relatively meager—a product mainly of India's old autarkic economic strategy—but the good news prospectively is that bilateral trade has increased sharply over the past few years. In 2004, U.S. merchandise exports to and imports from India are estimated to have totaled US$6.1 billion and US$15.5 billion respectively, making India the twenty-fourthlargest U.S. export market and the eighteenthlargest supplier of U.S. imports. In 2004, U.S. merchandise exports to India increased by 22.6 percent, over 2003, and imports by 18.4 percent. The United States also remains India's secondlargest source of FDI. U.S. cumulative FDI was US$4.1 billion in 2004, a 10.6 percent share of all such investment in India. Although these data suggest a dramatic improvement in U.S.-Indian economic ties, they nonetheless substantiate only very modest degrees of interdependence: American trade turnover with India still constitutes less than one percent of the United States' global trade; India's percentage share of U.S. imports still hovers at less than one percent as well.

This limited extent of interdependence has profound consequences. At a purely economic level, it implies that India still has not been able to utilize American resources as effectively as some other states, such as China, to elevate its level of growth. This, in turn, raises the issue of whether New Delhi might be better served by radically changing the strategy it has followed since the early 1990s, namely, the gradual, unilateralist approach to trade reform under which the focus remains on instituting step-by-step tariff reductions on merchandise, signing free-trade agreements with various developing countries, and participating actively in the World Trade Organization (WTO), but on the premise that India needs differential treatment in any multilateral agreement. This strategy has allowed India to maximize domestic autonomy and control, but it has produced policy uncertainty and increased incentives for backsliding. As a consequence, it has limited the utility of trade as a mechanism for spurring economic growth.

Pursuing a Bilateral Free-Trade Agreement: A Possible New Strategy

New Delhi should now consider whether a new strategy centered on a bilateral free-trade agreement with the United States ought to complement reliance on unilateral and WTO liberalization as a means of forcing major changes in domestic policies in order to spur economic growth. Many economists, including those otherwise supportive of global trade liberalization, often criticize such preferential trading agreements because, among other reasons, they encourage trade diversion, meaning that they divert trade from a more efficient supplier outside the free-trade area toward a less efficient supplier within it. This problem cannot be readily dismissed, but it needs to be examined in the U.S.-Indian case on a detailed sector-by-sector basis because a preferential trading agreement in that context could also produce offsetting trade-creating effects.

At any rate, India has already concluded that trade-creating advantages outweigh the problems of trade diversion in at least some specific cases. Consequently, New Delhi has begun to move down the road of preferential trade agreements, albeit in modest and hesitant ways, as exemplified by accords signed with Sri Lanka, Bhutan, and Thailand; the framework agreement with the Association of South East Asian Nations; and the South Asian Free Trade Area accord. In addition to a long-standing free-trade agreement with Nepal, New Delhi has explored similar partnerships with Chile, the South American economic union Mercosur, and South Africa. Given this shift in Indian policy, the renewed economic dialogue between Washington and New Delhi ought to closely examine a free-trade agreement precisely because it could function as an effective structural device by which the United States could advance the growth of Indian power, but through market mechanisms rather than centralized direction. Such an agreement would have great benefits for New Delhi insofar as it would enable India to exploit the welfare gains from trade while serving as "an effective mechanism for locking in reform policies, mobilizing domestic political support for liberalization, and spurring additional trade liberalization both multilaterally and bilaterally."[21]

A free-trade agreement between the United States and India would, therefore, do more to enhance the growth of Indian power—permanently—than many of the other instruments now being discussed between the two countries.

A free-trade agreement that boosted American investment in India would also have major—and reinforcing—political consequences. By making an important fraction of American employment and wealth creation dependent on Indian sources, many important and politically significant constituencies in the United States would acquire a new stake in India's stability, security and well-being. This fact would in actuality constrain Washington's ability to pursue policies vis-à-vis India's neighbors that competed with New Delhi's own interests, but this limitation would naturally decay in significance given the already strong congruence in U.S.-Indian political aims and the large and growing material benefits that would accrue to the United States as a result of expanded economic relations with India. A free-trade agreement between the United States and India would, therefore, do more to enhance the growth of Indian power—permanently—than many of the other instruments now being discussed between the two countries. Consequently, the best way the renewed economic dialogue could avoid the fate of its previous incarnations and advance the new U.S. goal of supporting the growth of Indian power would be to encourage progress toward a comprehensive free-trade accord, even if it were to exclude a few particularly sensitive areas and would be implemented only gradually, over the course of a couple of decades.

In recent years, India itself has intermittently proposed free-trade agreements with the United States, but has restricted these suggestions mainly to services. Such proposals, which appear selfserving in that they would permit New Delhi to secure guaranteed markets for outputs produced by its skilled, low-cost labor, are uninteresting to the United States because they do not provide compensating access for American goods to the Indian market. The fear of being overwhelmed by high-quality U.S. products—with all the associated consequences for domestic employment, resource allocation, and, ultimately, political survival —is why Indian leaders have shied away from comprehensive free-trade agreements involving the United States.

While the domestic costs of such arrangements would initially be high for Indian policy makers, there are nonetheless three reasons why New Delhi ought to consider reaching a free-trade accord with Washington. *First*, there is good economic analysis demonstrating that Indian gains deriving from preferential access to the United States, coupled with continuing domestic liberalization, are greater than those accruing from many alternative economic strategies, including current approaches, even when the disadvantages of trade diversion are taken into account. *Second*, because domestic reform is often difficult to implement in the face of objections by various rent-seeking constituencies —yet is vital to the continued growth of Indian power—a comprehensive free-trade agreement that forced further reform by means of binding external commitments would be a useful means of pushing change in the face of popular resistance. *Third*, a comprehensive free-trade agreement with the United States would require India to implement many painful internal reforms (that cannot be postponed interminably) as the price for constructing a more efficient and capable economy. But as Suman Bery, director-general of India's National Council of Applied Economic Research, has concluded, "If we are serious about liberalizing and becoming a global force to equal China, the idea of a comprehensive U.S.-India [free-trade agreement] has much to commend it."[22]

With these reasons in mind, India and the United States ought to use the economic dialogue to discuss a comprehensive free-trade agreement that could be implemented in a step-by-step fashion. The .first step could be to create several qualified export zones to expand both regional and bilateral trade. The second step could involve building upon this notion to implement a limited free-trade agreement in services. The third step might involve liberalized trade in manufactured goods, and the .final step would call for realizing, over a defined period, a comprehensive free-trade agreement that included liberalization of agriculture while incorporating the necessary safeguards and exclusions that might be necessary to make such an accord viable. In its .final form, a U.S.- Indian free trade agreement would not only impose symmetrical obligations on both countries but also—and more significantly—assist India with respect to competitive liberalization vis-àvis third parties that would likely beseech New Delhi for access comparable to that enjoyed by Americanfirms.

Achieving such a multistep agreement would b e difficult for both sides today. At a time when the U.S. economy is facing sluggish growth, especially in employment, American politicians are unlikely to be enthusiastic about a free-trade pact with India that front-loads many benefits to the Indian service sector. Indian politicians, too, although capable of appreciating the economic and political benefits of an appropriately structured and sequenced free-trade agreement with the United States, would likely be unnerved by the near-term political costs associated with the painful internal restructuring of the Indian economy that would result. Yet these difficulties notwithstanding, it is increasingly obvious that radically expanded U.S.- Indian trade would not only advance economic growth and consumer welfare in both countries but also rapidly enhance India's national power, now an objective of the Bush administration in addition to being a long-standing goal in New Delhi. For these reasons, if no other, a bilateral free trade agreement deserves new scrutiny in the U.S.-India economic dialogue.

Consistent with the larger effort to integrate the two economies, the United States should also endorse Indian membership in the Group of Eight and in the Asia-Pacific Economic Cooperation forum. Doing so would not only accelerate India's assimilation into the global economy but would serve the larger strategy of augmenting Indian power.

CONCLUSION: A TALE OF TWO CHALLENGES

Unlike his predecessors, President George W. Bush has demonstrated a strong desire to transform relations with India, guided by his administration's understanding of the geopolitical challenges likely to confront the United States in the twenty-First century. In this context, augmenting Indian power is judged to be essential to U.S. interests because it permits Washington to "pursue a balance-of-power strategy among those major rising powers and key regional states in Asia which are not part of the existing U.S. alliance structure—including China, India, and a currently weakened Russia," a strategy that "seeks to prevent any one of these [countries] from effectively threatening the security of another [or that of the United States] while simultaneously preventing any combination of these [entities] from 'bandwagoning' to undercut critical U.S. strategic interests in Asia."[23]

Unlike his predecessors, President George W. Bush has demonstrated a strong desire to transform relations with India, guided by his administration's understanding of the geopolitical challenges likely to confront the United States in the twenty-First century.

Since the United States is unlikely to be challenged by any peer competitor in the near term, however, the myriad policy changes sought by New Delhi through the bilateral dialogues on energy security, strategic cooperation, and economic engagement are unlikely to gain much traction in the absence of concerted direction by President Bush himself. The fact that India's economic growth today is also self-directed and likely to continue autonomously—barring some catastrophe such as a pandemic or a nuclear war—ironically weakens the incentives for urgent action by the Bush administration.

Finally, the enormous difficulty of granting New Delhi an exception to existing U.S. policy, law, and international regime commitments, which would require congressional and perhaps even public consent in the United States, could discourage even otherwise motivated officials from pursuing what may be their preferred courses of action on many issues relating to India.

All things considered, therefore, there is a real risk that even the Bush administration, no matter how determined it may be to support the growth of Indian power, could end up making some modest policy changes as a token of its good intentions while failing to move as rapidly or as extensively on the more difficult policy transformations the government of Prime Minister Manmohan Singh considers necessary to the success of a new, sturdy, bilateral relationship.

The most likely danger confronting the Bush administration's new strategy toward India, therefore, may not be that it ends up being so wildly successful that it threatens other U.S. interests, but that it peters out prematurely—with serious consequences for both New Delhi and Washington. This risk ought to concern President Bush not only because it bears on the future of what has been perhaps his most undeniable foreign policy achievement but because it has potentially grave implications for the future balance of power in Asia, management of the United States-India-Pakistan triangle, and Washington's ability to in-.fiance its South Asian partners during a crisis. It is not lost on policy makers in New Delhi that the Bush administration's latest pronouncement about its decision to boost Indian power, while certainly welcome, remains—at least at the moment—an innovation at the level of intention rather than at the level of policy. Cynics within the Indian cabinet have privately expressed the opinion that, while the new U.S. approach actually provides Islamabad with airplanes, all that New Delhi has received thus far are eloquent words. Although this judgment is premature and unduly harsh, it highlights one important reality that the administration ought not to lose sight of: the advances pertaining to India have occurred so far either at an ideational level or in the realm of process, but they have not yet translated into concrete policy changes that produce fresh material gains for New Delhi.

The new willingness to coproduce military equipment, for example, which some Bush administration officials advance as major evidence refuting the cynics' claims, simply does not have the same resonance in New Delhi that it may possess in Washington. While Indian leaders, if pressed, will concede that this U.S. offer represents a meaningful solution to their concerns about constricted access to advanced weapons systems and the reliability of supplies, they also reiterate that India's growing economic strength now permits it to secure a variety of comparable defense equipment on similar terms in the international market. More to the point, however, they do not see military technology as constituting the *principal* means of fulfilling their country's desire for greatness. This need can only be satisfied by more liberal access to a variety of civilian high technologies, such as nuclear energy, satellite components, and advanced industrial equipment, which hold the promise of helping India attain the even higher levels of economic growth necessary for rapid development. To be sure, India's continued rise will depend substantially on its own choices with respect to economic reform. But U.S. decisions about liberalizing access to critical technologies will make an important difference in the pace at which India grows and the ease with which it develops as a major industrial power. In a competitive international system, where relative growth matters more than absolute growth, U.S. contributions that help India accelerate development while ensuring national security—through different kinds of high technology —may turn out to be consequential after all.

The greatest risk to the new Bush strategy, therefore, is that the administration may be unable to realize the policy changes needed to make increased Indian access to such technologies possible. This outcome could occur either because the United States concluded that creating exceptional carve-outs for India was neither possible nor worth the cost in relation to other objectives, or because India failed to make itself sufficiently useful to Washington to justify the enormous political investment that would be required to craft an accommodation that satisfied New Delhi. If that eventually turns out to be the case, the United States and India will not only have lost a golden opportunity to forge a durable strategic partnership, but the cynics within the Indian polity will have been proven right. The administration's claim to support the growth of Indian power will be viewed merely as lofty rhetoric, full of sound and fury, signifying nothing—or even worse, as cunning manipulation designed to pacify India while the United States proceeds with its plans to rearm Pakistan. If this dismal outcome is to be avoided, and a real transformation of those policies concretely affecting India is to occur, the principals in the State Department and the White House will have to exercise the same kind of political initiative that was displayed when the new U.S. strategy toward South Asia was crafted earlier this year.

While these challenges facing the United States are onerous enough, they represent only half of the story. The other half pertains to the challenges facing India. Given the difficult changes in U.S. policy and law required to satisfy New Delhi, it will become increasingly obvious over time that the Bush administration will have diminishing incentives to accept these burdens if India is unable to demonstrate a new willingness to ally itself with American purposes. While the United States is likely of its own accord to make some changes that satisfy India, it is unlikely to pursue "maximizing" strategies that reach for the full extent of policy transformation unless New Delhi responds with robust demonstrations of support for U.S. interests. At the moment, it is simply unclear whether New Delhi can meet this test. India is a large, proud, populous country with complex ideologies and diverse domestic constituencies, each expressing its preferences through vigorous representative institutions and a feisty civil society, so any Indian government will be constrained in its ability to express support for U.S. policies, especially controversial ones. India's traditional—and enduring—preference for strategic autonomy, which includes the right to choose both the friends it keeps and the policies it follows, further limits the kind of geopolitical collaboration Washington is likely to seek in order to justify the changes in U.S. policy that would favor India in exceptional ways. Taken together, these factors could prevent New Delhi from pursuing the kind of actions that would find favor in Washington, and, as a consequence, limit U.S. incentives to pursue the policy changes of most interest to India.

Unless Indian security managers, therefore, make conscious efforts to shape their national policies to promote at least tacit coordination with, if not extensive support for, U.S. goals, the strategic partnership that both sides seek will remain elusive, and, by extension, the policy changes of importance to India will defy realization. None of this is meant to suggest that the United States expects India to support U.S. interests unquali-.edly, or invariably, as the price of policy change. The Bush administration understands clearly that differences in perception, and often in interests, will continue to characterize this bilateral relationship, as it frequently does others. Accordingly, what Washington hopes for—at the very least—is that New Delhi becomes sensitive enough to U.S. concerns to avoid reflexive opposition when no vital Indian interests are at immediate risk. For example, most issues at the United Nations, where India invariably finds itself on the opposite side of the United States, fall within this category.

Beyond these lesser but nonetheless real irritants, the Bush administration hopes that India will seek—and .find—ways to harmonize its own political strategies with those of the United States so as to attain common goals, something that has been more the exception than the norm in previous decades. Given India's desire to preserve its "nonaligned" character (despite the absence of those power blocs that originally gave rise to this preference), the United States would welcome "strategic coordination"—meaning implicit rather than overt collaboration—as a means of achieving political harmony. The estrangement of the past, however, ensures that the obstacles to fashioning a new relationship of this kind cannot be underestimated. Yet if the goal of fundamental policy change in the United States is to be achieved, Indian decision makers will be squarely challenged to display the same imagination they demand of their U.S. counterparts, and to fashion supportive policies that increase Washington's incentives to support Indian preferences in the three diplomatic dialogues scheduled to occur in the months ahead.

NOTES

1. "India, USA and the World," Remarks by Indian Prime Minister Atal Bihari Vajpayee at the Asia Society, New York, September 28, 1998, available at www.asiasociety. org/speeches/vajpayee.html.
2. "Joint Statement between the United States of America and the Republic of India," November 9, 2001, available at www.whitehouse.gov/news/releases/2001/11/200111 09-10.html.
3. Thomas R. Pickering, "U.S. Policy in South Asia: The Road Ahead," address to the Foreign Policy Institute, South Asia Program, Paul H. Nitze School of Advanced International Studies, Johns Hopkins University, Washington, D.C., April 27, 2000, available at www.fas. org/news/pakistan/2000/000427_pickering_sa.htm.
4. Secretary of State Condoleezza Rice, "Remarks at Sophia University," Tokyo, March 19, 2005, available at www. state.gov/secretary/rm/ 2005/43655.htm.
5. Secretary of State Condoleezza Rice, "Interview with Shirvaj Prasad of NDTV," New Delhi, India, March 16, 2005, available at www.state.gov/secretary/ rm/2005/43511.htm.

6. Amit Baruah, "We Are Disappointed: Manmohan," *The Hindu*, March 26, 2005, available at www.hindu. com/2005/03/26/stories/2005032606320100.htm.
7. U.S. Department of State, "Background Briefing by Administration Officials on U.S.-South Asia Relations," March 25, 2005, available at www.state.gov/r/pa/prs/ ps/2005/43853.htm.
8. Frank Carlucci, Robert Hunter, and Zalmay Khalilzad, eds., *Taking Charge: A Bipartisan Report to the President Elect on Foreign Policy and National Security—Papers* (Santa Monica, Calif.: RAND, 2000), p. 88.
9. U.S. Department of State, "Background Briefing," note 7.
10. Siddharth Varadarajan, "F-16s for Pakistan Will Fuel Arms Race," *The Hindu*, March 27, 2005, available at www. hindu.com/2005/03/27/stories/2005032707050100.htm.
11. Secretary of State Condoleezza Rice, Remarks with Indian Foreign Minister Natwar Singh, Hyderabad House, New Delhi, India, March 16, 2005, available at www.state. gov/secretary/rm/2005/43490.htm.
12. U.S. Department of State, "Background Briefing," note 7. 13 Secretary of State Condoleezza Rice, "Interview With Raj Chengappa of *India Today*," New Delhi, India, March 16, 2005, available at ww.state.gov/secretary/ rm/2005/43626.htm.
14. World Nuclear Association, "Thorium," Information and Issue Briefs, November 2004, available at www.worldnuclear. org/info/inf62.htm.
15. George Perkovich, Jessica T. Mathews, Joseph Cirincione, Rose Gottemoeller, and Jon B. Wolfsthal, *Universal Compliance: A Strategy for Nuclear Security* (Washington, D.C.: Carnegie Endowment for International Peace, 2005), p. 48.
16. Secretary of State Condoleezza Rice, "Remarks with Indian Minister of External Affairs Natwar Singh Following Meeting," Department of State, Washington, D.C., April 14, 2005, available at www.state.gov/secretary/rm/2005/44662.htm.

17. John R. Bolton, "An All-Out War on Proliferation," *The Financial Times,* September 7, 2004, available at www. acronym.org.uk/docs/0409/doc01.htm.
18. Richard Ullman, "The Covert French Connection," *Foreign Policy* 75 (Summer 1989), pp. 3–33.
19. Robert D. Blackwill, "A New Deal for New Delhi," *The Wall Street Journal,* March 21, 2005, p. A16.
20. Kenneth I. Juster, "Cybersecurity: A Key to U.S.-India Trade," keynote address to the India-U.S. Information Security Summit 2004, New Delhi, India, October 12, 2004, available at www.state.gov/p/sa/rls/rm/37039.htm.
21. Robert Z. Lawrence and Rajesh Chada, "Should a U.S.- India FTA Be Part of India's Trade Strategy?" in Suman Bery, Barry Bosworth, and Arvind Panagariya, eds., *India Policy Forum* 2004, Volume 1 (Washington, D.C., and New Delhi, India: Brookings Institution Press and National Council for Applied Economic Research, 2005), p. 3. This section draws greatly from Lawrence and Chada.
22. Suman Bery, "Needed: A U.S.-India FTA," *Rediff.com,* Business, November 9, 2004, available at http://us.rediff. com/money/2004/nov/09guest1.htm.
23. Zalmay Khalilzad, David Orletsky, Jonathan Pollack, Kevin Pollpeter, Angel Rabasa, David Shlapak, Abram Shulsky, and Ashley J. Tellis, *The United States and Asia: Toward a New U.S. Strategy and Force Posture* (Santa Monica, Calif.: RAND, 2001), p. 47.

ABOUT THE AUTHOR

Ashley J. Tellis is a senior associate at the Carnegie Endowment for International Peace in Washington,

D.C. Previously, he served as senior adviser to the ambassador at the embassy of the United States in India.

He also served on the National Security Council staff as special assistant to the president and senior director for strategic planning and Southwest Asia. Before his government service, he was for eight years a senior policy analyst at RAND and professor of policy analysis at the RAND graduate school. He is the author of *India's Emerging Nuclear Posture,* coauthor of *China's Grand Strategy: Past, Present, and Future,* and has recently edited *Strategic Asia 2004–05: Confronting Terrorism in the Pursuit of Power.*

CARNEGIE ENDOWMENT FOR INTERNATIONAL PEACE

The Carnegie Endowment for International Peace is a private, nonpro.t organization dedicated to advancing cooperation between nations and promoting active international engagement by the United States. Founded in 1910, Carnegie is nonpartisan and dedicated to achieving practical results.

Through research, publishing, convening, and, on occasion, creating new institutions and international networks, Endowment associates shape fresh policy approaches. Their interests span geographic regions and the relations between governments, business, international organizations, and civil society, focusing on the economic, political, and technological forces driving global change. Through its Carnegie Moscow Center, the Endowment helps to develop a tradition of public policy analysis in the states of the former Soviet Union and to improve relations between Russia and the United States. The Endowment publishes FOREIGN POLICY, one of the world's leading magazines of international politics and economics, which reaches readers in more than 120 countries and in several languages.

For more information about the Carnegie Endowment, visit www.CarnegieEndowment.org.

India Research Press

India Research Press is a collectively run book publisher with active support of Authors and Editors. Since our founding in 1999, we have tried to meet the needs of readers who are exploring, or are committed to the politics of change.

Our goal is to publish books that encourage critical thinking and constructive action on the key political, cultural, social, economic and ecological issues shaping life in the Indian Sub-continent and in the world. In this way, we hope to give expression to a wide diversity of democratic and social movements.

India Research Press publishes Original works-as well as-works under Rights with various University and Academic institutions throughout the world. This is their third joint publication with the Carnegie Endowment for International Peace.

For more information, visit

www.indiaresearchpress.com